S0-BAG-246

3 5674 00302121 0

MICHIGAN VOICES

Michigan *Voices*

OUR STATE'S HISTORY IN THE WORDS OF THE PEOPLE WHO LIVED IT

Compiled and edited
by Joe Grimm

DETROIT
FREE PRESS

WAYNE STATE
UNIVERSITY PRESS

R977.4
M6809
c.1

Editor: Joe Grimm
Designer: Suzanne Yeager
Copy Editor: Kate Ransdell
Photo copy work: Ed Haun, Helen McQuerry, John Luke
Project Coordinator: Michele Kapecky
Proofreader: Marcia Abramson

On the cover: Abolitionist Elizabeth Margaret Chandler. Excerpts from her letters are on Page 43.

Published by the Detroit Free Press
Detroit, Michigan
and
Wayne State University Press
Detroit, Michigan
1987

All rights reserved. No part of this book may be reproduced or transmitted in any form or by any means, electronic or mechanical, including photocopying, recording or by an information storage and retrieval system, without permission of the publisher, except where permitted by law.

Library of Congress Cataloging in Publication
Number 87-071542

ISBN 0-8143-1967-X (cl)
0-8143-1968-8 (pbk)

CHASE BRANCH LIBRARY
17731 W. SEVEN MILE
DETROIT. MICH. 48235

JUN '88

CH

Michigan Voices

Introduction

Most history books resound with the words of the powerful and prominent. This book is a hubbub of voices great and small. "Michigan Voices" unites loggers and lakers, miners and merchants in a patchwork portrait of a crazy-quilt state. Never a place to be confined by one label or description, Michigan has a history that rings as loudly in the songs of its forests as it does in the shouts of its factories.

Michigan's diverse voices have been heard in the pages of the Detroit Free Press since 1831, six years before statehood, and the Free Press published these accounts to celebrate Michigan's 150th anniversary.

Readers submitted hundreds of old family diaries, letters and photographs for the series. Many had never been seen outside a small circle of family or friends and nearly half the material in "Michigan Voices" had not been published before.

These stories, with accounts from archives and libraries, tell Michigan's history in the unvarnished words of so-called ordinary people. They wrote or spoke about the events around them, without hindsight or pretension. They told of dreams, hopes, fears and perceptions that can have more influence over our actions than reality.

Open "Michigan Voices" and you open an invitation. It is an invitation to visit Michigan's past, to hear the extraordinary in ordinary lives and to see that each of us is a maker, not just a spectator, of history.

Scores of voices speaking over a span of several hundred years are bound to bring inconsistencies to such conventions as punctuation and spelling. These have been standardized to eliminate distractions. For the same reason, there are no ellipses to show how these accounts have been condensed. Insertions that help the accounts along are in parentheses. We have tried to remain faithful to each original and to say where it can be found.

— Joe Grimm

Acknowledgments

"Michigan Voices," like Michigan history, is a group effort. People whose letters and diaries trace a rich story in honest language wrote it. Children, grandchildren and strangers who tucked those accounts into drawers and shoeboxes preserved it. The hundreds of people throughout Michigan and across the country who sent in bits of family history, encouragement, criticism and suggestions shaped it.

The collection would be incomplete without the stewards of Michigan's past who work in archives, libraries and historical societies. They include: Alice Dalligan, Mary Karshner and Margaret Ward at the Detroit Public Library's Burton Historical Collection; Nancy Bartlett and Matt Schaefer at the University of Michigan's Bentley Historical Library; Thomas Featherstone at the Archives of Labor and Urban Affairs, Wayne State University; Cynthia Read-Miller at the collections of Henry Ford Museum and Greenfield Village, and John Curry at the Michigan State Archives.

Michigan State University history professor Justin Kestenbaum read a very rough manuscript and suggested many improvements.

Finally, this collection would not be in your hands without the help of my critic, friend and wife, Debbie. She took care of our two rambunctious sons while I hid out in the stillness of libraries, and then read the accounts and offered suggestions and support.

Each of these people helped make "Michigan Voices" better. Its successes are theirs; any shortcomings are mine alone.

— *Joe Grimm*

Into
the wilderness

" . . . every child of the forest was observing and living under the precepts which their forefathers taught them."
— Andrew J. Blackbird

1800s *'Our lodges had no fastenings'*

Michigan's native people lived simply, happily

There are no written accounts of what life was like for Michigan's first people. They wrote no letters, kept no diaries and no one wrote down their histories until the Europeans arrived. In 1887 Andrew J. Blackbird, the son of an Ottawa chief and a one-time student at Eastern Michigan University, denounced many of the accounts as being "far from credible" and told his own story of life for Native Americans before Michigan became a state.

In my first recollection of L'Arbre Croche (now Harbor Springs), which is 60 years ago, there was nothing but small shrubbery here and there in small patches, such as wild cherry trees, but the most of it was grassy plain; and such an abundance of wild strawberries, raspberries and blackberries that they fairly perfumed the air of the whole coast with fragrant scent of ripe fruit. The wild pigeons and every variety of feathered songsters filled all the groves, and in these waters the fishes were so plentiful that as you lift up the anchor stone of your net in the morning, your net would be so loaded with delicious whitefish as to fairly float with all its weight of the sinkers. Then I never knew my people to want for anything to eat or to wear. I thought, and yet I may be mistaken, that my people were very happy in those days.

Swearing or profanity was never heard among the Ottawa and Chippewa tribes of Indians, and not even found in their language. Scarcely any drunkenness, only once in a great while the old folks used to have a kind of short spree, particularly when there was any special occasion of a great feast going on.

And we always rested in perfect safety at night in our dwellings, and the doorways of our lodges had no fastenings to them, but simply a frail mat or a blanket was hung over our doorways, which might be easily pushed or thrown (to) one side without any noise if theft or any other mischief was intended. But we were not afraid for any such thing to happen to us, because we knew that every child of the forest was observing and living under the precepts which their forefathers taught them.

In the former times or before the Indians were Christianized, when a young man came to be a fit age to get married, he did not trouble himself about what girl he should have for his wife; but the parents of the young man did this part of the business. And after selecting some particular girl among their neighbors, they would make up quite (a) large package of presents and then go to the parents of the girl and demand the daughter for their son's wife.

If the old folks say yes, then they would fetch the girl right along to their son and tell him, "We have brought this girl as your wife so long as you live; now take her, cherish her and be kind to her so long as you live."

From Andrew J. Blackbird's "History of the Ottawa and Chippewa Indians of Michigan," published by the Ypsilanti Auxiliary of the Women's National Indian Association, Ypsilanti, 1887: pages 10-18.

From "History of the Ottawa and Chippewa Indians of Michigan"
Andrew J. Blackbird, whose Ottawa name, Mack-aw-de-be-nessy, meant Black Hawk.

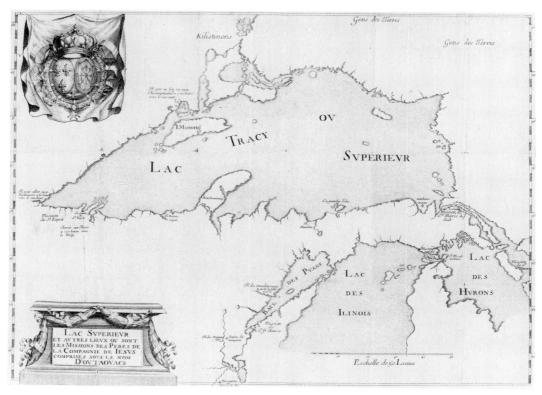

William L. Clements Library, University of Michigan

Based in part on Father Claude Allouez' travels, the Jesuits in 1671 made this map, which shows "Lake Tracy or Superior."

1665 *'The savages revere this lake'*

French missionary seeks souls on Superior's shores

Father Claude Allouez, a French Jesuit, became one of the first Europeans to see the Great Lakes when he traveled by canoe through northern Lake Huron and Lake Superior in 1665. He described the area in letters to his superiors in France.

Toward the beginning of September, after coasting along the shores of the Lake of the Hurons, we reached the Sault; for such is the name given to a half-league of rapids that are encountered in a beautiful river which unites two great lakes — that of the Hurons and Lake Superior.

This river is pleasing, not only on account of the islands intercepting its course and the great bays bordering it, but because of the fishing and hunting, which are excellent there. We sought a resting place for the night on one of these islands, where our savages thought they would find provision for supper upon their arrival; for, as soon as they landed, they put the kettle on the fire, expecting to see the canoe laden with fish the moment the net was cast into the water. But God chose to punish their presumption and deferred giving any food to the starving men until the following day.

On the second of September, then, after clearing this Sault — which is not a waterfall, but merely a very swift current impeded by several rocks — we entered Lake Superior, which will henceforth bear Monsieur de Tracy's name, in recognition of indebtedness to him on the part of the people of those regions. (Sent by Louis XIV to fight the Iroquois, Alexandre de Prouville, Marquis de Tracy, secured a treaty opening the lower lakes.)

The form of this lake is nearly that of a bow, the southern shore being much curved and the northern nearly straight. Fish are abundant there and of excellent quality; while the water is so clear and pure that objects at the bottom can be seen to the depth of six brasses (about 36 feet).

The savages revere this lake as a divinity and offer it sacrifices, whether on account of its size, or because of its goodness in furnishing fish for the sustenance of all these tribes, in default of game, which is scarce in the neighborhood.

One often finds at the bottom of the water pieces of pure copper, of 10 and 20 livres' (pounds) weight. I have several times seen such pieces in the savages' hands; and, since they are superstitious, they keep them as so many divinities or as presents which the gods dwelling beneath the water have given them and on which their welfare is to depend. For this reason they preserve these pieces of copper, wrapped up, among their most precious possessions. Some have kept them for more than 50 years; others have had them in their families from time immemorial and cherish them as household gods.

This lake is, furthermore, the resort of 12 or 15 distinct nations, and they all betake themselves either to the best parts of the shore for fishing or to the islands, which are scattered in great numbers all over the lake. These peoples' motive in repairing hither is partly to obtain food by fishing and partly to transact their petty trading with one another when they meet. But God's purpose was to facilitate the proclaiming of the gospel to wandering and vagrant tribes.

On this trip and subsequent trips, Allouez mapped out all of Lake Superior and the northern parts of lakes Huron and Michigan. Europeans did not explore the southern lakes until after Allouez and others had traveled all along the upper lakes. From Reuben Gold Thwaites, "Jesuit Relations and Allied Documents," (73 vols., 1896-1901) Vol. 50, Burrows Brothers Co., Cleveland, 1900: pages 249-271.

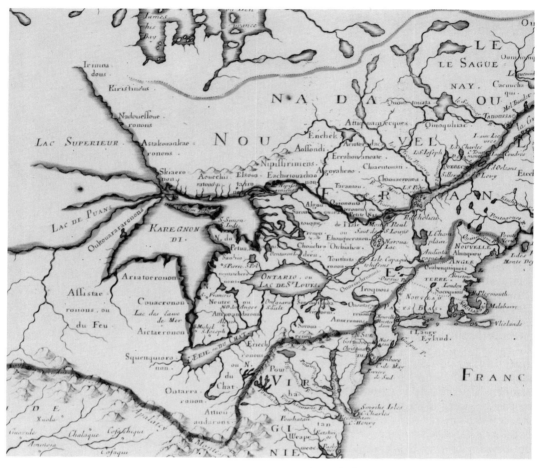

William L. Clements Library, University of Michigan

Nicholas Sanson's 1656 map of the Great Lakes area was used widely until the end of the century.

1669 'A place that is very remarkable'

Missionaries shatter stone idol to spread their own religion

In 1669, trader and explorer Adrien Jolliet made the first recorded trip by a European to Michigan's Lower Peninsula. The next year, Sulpician missionaries Francois Dollier de Casson and Rene de Brehan de Galinee followed Jolliet's map to canoe north through Lake Huron. These excerpts from Galinee's report are the first written descriptions of the Detroit River, Lake St. Clair and the St. Clair River.

We pursued our course accordingly towards the west and, after making about 100 leagues on Lake Erie, arrived at the place where the Lake of the Hurons, otherwise called the Fresh Water Sea of the Hurons or Michigans, discharges into this lake. This outlet (the Detroit River) is perhaps half a league in width and turns sharp to the northeast, so that we were almost retracing our path. At the end of six leagues, we discovered a place that is very remarkable and held in great veneration by all the Indians of these countries, because of a stone idol that nature has formed there. (This was very close to or within the present boundaries of Detroit.)

I leave you to imagine whether we avenged upon this idol, which the Iroquois had strongly recommended us to honor, the loss of our chapel. We attributed to it even the dearth of provisions from which we had hitherto suffered. I consecrated one of my axes to break this god of stone and then, having yoked our canoes together, we carried the largest pieces to the middle of the river and threw all the rest also into the water.

At the end of four leagues we entered a small lake, about 10 leagues in length and almost as many in width, called by (Nicholas) Sanson the Salt Water Lake (Lake St. Clair), but we saw no sign of salt in this lake.

We entered the outlet of Lake Michigan (present-day Lake Huron), which is not quite a quarter of a league in width.

Although this lake is as large as the Caspian Sea, and much larger than Lake Erie, storms do not arise in it either so violent or so long, because it is not very deep. (In reality, Erie is much shallower than Huron.)

The nation of the Salteaux, or Ojibways, live from the melting of the snows until the beginning of winter on the bank of a river nearly half-a-league wide and three leagues long, by which Lake Superior falls into the Lake of the Hurons. This river forms at this place a rapid so teeming with fish, called whitefish, that the Indians could easily catch enough to feed 10,000 men.

It is true the fishing is so difficult that only Indians can carry it on. No Frenchman has hitherto been able to succeed at it, nor any other Indian than those of this tribe, who are used to this kind of fishing from an early age. But, in short, this fish is so cheap that they give 10 or 12 of them for four fingers of tobacco. Each weighs six or seven pounds, but is so big and so delicate that I know of no fish that approaches it. Meat is so cheap here that for a pound of glass beads I had (a large quantity) of fat entrails of moose, which is the best morsel of the animal. This shows how many the people kill. It is at these places that one gets a beaver robe for a fathom of tobacco, sometimes for a quarter of a pound of powder, sometimes for six knives, sometimes for a fathom of blue beads, etc. This is why the French go there, notwithstanding the frightful difficulties that are encountered.

From Louise Phelps Kellogg, "Early Narratives of the Northwest," Charles Scribner's Sons, New York, 1917: pages 203-207.

15

Antoine de la Mothe Cadillac, as depicted by Julie Paul for "Cadillac and the Founding of Detroit," published for the Detroit Historical Society by Wayne State University Press in 1976.

1700 *'To tame them and set them free'*

Cadillac says 'savage maidens' will prefer Frenchmen

Antoine de la Mothe Cadillac, a French military officer in his 40s, saw opportunity on the Detroit riverbank in 1700. He believed France could use this position as a choke hold on the interior of the continent and cut off British trade. On Oct. 18, 1700, he wrote a letter to his superiors in France outlining his plans for establishing a colony on the Detroit River.

It is my duty to give you an exact account of all that I have done regarding the establishment of Detroit.

It is an incontestable fact that the strength of the savages lies in the remoteness of the French and that ours increases against them with our proximity. For it is certain that, with a little Indian corn, these people have no difficulty in traversing 200 leagues to come and take someone's life by stealth; and when we want to get to their lands, we are obliged to provide ourselves with stores of all kinds and to make great preparations, which involves the king in extraordinary expenses, and always with very little effect since it is like beating drums to catch hares.

But, on the contrary, when we are the neighbors of that tribe and are within easy reach of them, they will be kept in awe.

In order to succeed thoroughly, it would be well, in my opinion, to adopt the following measures.

● To go and station ourselves with a hundred men, one-half of whom should be soldiers and the other Canadians.

● The year after, the fort being secure from insult, it is well to allow 20 or 30 families to settle there.

● It is no less necessary that the king should send 200 picked men who should, as far as may be, be of different trades and also rather young.

● It is not advisable that I, any more than the other officers, soldiers and inhabitants, should do any trade with savages, but to unite this business to that of the general company which is formed.

● We must establish at this post missionaries of different communities, with orders in particular to teach the young savages the French language, (that) being the only means to civilize and humanize them. We take wild beasts at their birth, birds in their nests, to tame them and set them free.

● The third or fourth year we shall be able to set Ursulines there, or other nuns.

● It would be important that there should be a hospital for sick or infirm savages, for there is nothing more urgent for gaining their friendship than the care taken of them in their illness.

● It would be absolutely necessary also to allow the soldiers and Canadians to marry the savage maidens when they have been instructed in religion and know the French language, because they always prefer a Frenchman for a husband to any savage whatever.

● Marriages of this kind will strengthen the friendship of these tribes, as the alliances of the Romans perpetuated peace with the Sabines through the intervention of the women whom the former had taken from the others.

The next year, 1701, Cadillac founded the City of Detroit on the banks of the river. King Louis XIV appointed him governor of Louisiana in 1711, but Cadillac failed to establish a viable settlement there. He retired to France in 1716 and died there in 1730. From "Michigan Pioneer and Historical Collections," (40 vols., 1877-1929) Vol. 33, Michigan Pioneer and Historical Society, Lansing, 1904: pages 96-101.

1763 *'Drive from your land those dogs'*

Pontiac fans flames of revolt with Master of Life legend

It had been just two months since the French ceded control of the Great Lakes area to the British early in 1763. The area's native people, forced off their traditional lands by growing numbers of traders and settlers and abandoned by their French allies, were infuriated that Britain was now cutting back on customary payments of gifts. Several hundred Indians gathered on the Ecorse River south of Detroit on April 27, 1763. At that meeting, Ottawa Chief Pontiac told a legend. Crafted to kindle resistance to the British, the tale told of a Delaware Indian who traveled to paradise and received a message from the Master of Life.

God said, "I am the maker of heaven and Earth, the trees, lakes, rivers, men, and all that thou seest or hast seen on the Earth or in the heavens; and because I love you, you must do my will; you must also avoid that which I hate; I hate you to drink as you do, until you lose your reason; I wish you not to fight one another; you take two wives or run after other people's wives; you do wrong. I hate such conduct; you should have but one wife, and keep her until death. When you go to war, you juggle, you sing the medicine song, thinking you speak to me; you deceive yourselves; it is to the Manito that you speak; he is a wicked spirit who induces you to evil, and for want of knowing me, you listen to him.

"The land on which you are, I have made for you, not for others: Wherefore do you suffer the whites to dwell upon your lands? Can you not do without them? I know that those (the French) whom you call the children of your great father (King Louis XV) supply your wants. But were you not wicked as you are, you would not need them. You might live as you did before you knew them. Before those whom you call your brothers (the French) had arrived, did not your bow and arrow maintain you? You needed neither gun, powder, nor any other object. The flesh of animals was your food, their skins your raiment. But when I saw you inclined to evil, I removed the animals into the depths of the forests, that you might depend on your brothers for your necessaries (and) for your clothing. Again become good and do my will, and I will send animals for your sustenance. I do not, however, forbid (letting) among you your father's children (the French); I love them, they know me, they pray to me; I supply their wants, and give them that which they bring to you. Not so with these (the British) who come to trouble your possessions. Drive them away; wage war against them. I love them not. They know me not. They are my enemies, they are your brothers' enemies. Send them back to the lands I have made for them. Let them remain there.

"Drive from your lands those dogs in red clothing; they are only an injury to you. When you want anything, apply to me, as your brothers do, and I will give to both."

The story helped fan the Great Lakes tribes into their last great uprising, "Pontiac's Conspiracy." They conquered all British forts in the West except Pitt, Niagara and Detroit, but gradually gave them up as France withdrew from the region and the French-Indian alliance crumbled. From Henry R. Schoolcraft, "The Myth of Hiawatha and Other Oral Legends, Mythological and Allegoric, of the North American Indians," Avery Color Studios, AuTrain, Mich., 1984: pages 201 and 202.

Detroit Public Library

Chief Pontiac, based on the only original painting known.

1763 *'Hatchets hid under . . . blankets'*

British lose Fort Michilimackinac to a Chippewa ambush

After an unsuccessful siege at Detroit, Ottawa Chief Pontiac sent runners to urge his allies to attack other British forts in the West. On June 2, 1763, Chippewa braves played a ball game outside Fort Michilimackinac. When one threw the ball into the fort, they took weapons that Chippewa women were hiding under blankets and rushed into the fort. Captured post commandant Capt. George Etherington was one of 13 men who had been handed over to the Ottawas when he described the attack and its aftermath. This letter, written 10 days after the attack, was sent to Maj. Henry Gladwin, the British commandant at Detroit, by canoe.

The Chippewas who live in a plain near this fort assembled to play ball, as they had done almost every day since their arrival. They played from morning till noon, then, throwing their ball close to the gate and observing Lt. (William) Leslye and me a few paces out of it, they came behind us, seized and carried us into the woods. In the meantime, the rest rushed into the fort, where they found their squaws, whom they had previously planted there, with their hatchets hid under their blankets, which they took and in an instant killed Lt. (John) Jemay and 15 rank and file, and a trader named Tracy; they wounded two and took the rest of the garrison prisoners, five of which they have since killed.

They made prisoners of all the English traders and robbed them of everything they had, but offered no violence to any of the persons and properties of the Frenchmen.

When the massacre was over, (trader Charles) Langlade and Farti, the interpreter, came down to the place where Lt. Leslye and me were prisoners, and their

giving themselves as security to return us when demanded, they obtained leave for us to go to the fort under a guard of savages. This gave time to send for the Ottawas, who came down on the first notice and were very much displeased at what the Chippewas had done.

Since their arrival the Ottawas have done everything in their power to serve us, and I have now with me Lt. Leslye and 11 privates. The other four of the garrison who are yet living remain in the hands of the Chippewas.

The Chippewas, who are superior in numbers to the Ottawas, have declared in council to them that if they do not remove us out of the fort, that they will cut off all communication to this post; by which means all the convoys of merchants from Montreal, Labay, St. Joseph and the upper posts would perish, but if the news of your posts being attacked, which they say was the reason they took up the hatchet here, be false, and you can send up a strong reinforcement with provisions, etc., and accompanied by some of your savages, I believe the post might be re-established again. Since this affair happened, two canoes arrived from Montreal which put it in my power to make a present to the Ottawa nation, who very well deserve anything that can be done for them.

The Ottawas say they will take Lt. Leslye, me and the 11 men up to their village and there keep us until they hear what is done at your post, they having sent this canoe for that purpose.

The Ottawas took Etherington and his party to L'Arbre Croche and then to Montreal, where they released them. From "Michigan Pioneer and Historical Collections," (40 vols., 1877-1929) Vol. 27, Michigan Pioneer and Historical Society, Lansing, 1897: pages 631 and 632.

Michigan Bell Telephone

British soldiers watch outside Fort Michilimackinac as a Chippewa brave hurls a ball over the wall in this painting by Robert Thom.

1781 *'Causing them to war'*

Spanish flag flies over Michigan for a single day

Don Francisco Cruzat, Spanish commandant at St. Louis on the Mississippi River, explained the reasons behind one of the more bizarre invasions of the Revolutionary War in this Jan. 10, 1781, letter to Bernardo de Galvez, Spanish governor of Louisiana. Cruzat was about to send 60 men in the dead of winter to attack the unprotected British Fort St. Joseph, near southern Lake Michigan. Far from England's war with the American rebels, the fort had been all but abandoned.

My Dear Sir:

On the 26th of last month the (Milwaukee Indian) chief, El Heturno, arrived, bringing me news of the destruction (by the English) of a detachment of 17 Frenchmen (allies of the Spanish) who had set out for the purpose of going to take possession of the Fort of San Joseph. In (the fort) there are four persons commissioned by the English with 17 men and a considerable quantity of all sorts of merchandise, which they use only to purchase maize and different kinds of provisions from the neighboring Indians.

The urging of the Indian Heturno, both on his account and in behalf of Naquiguen (another Milwaukee chief), that I should make an expedition against the English of the Fort of San Joseph compelled me to arrange for a detachment of 60 volunteers (to raid the fort).

Indeed, it has been indispensable for me to take this step.

FIRST. For me not to have consented to the petition of El Heturno and Naquiguen would have been to demonstrate to them our weakness and to make evident our inadequate forces.

SECOND. To go to San Joseph and seize the fort, the merchandise and the provisions

Dominic Trupiano/Detroit Free Press

would have the effect of terrorizing the surrounding nations (of pro-British Indians).

With the savages it is always necessary, in order to preserve oneself from their destructive inclinations, to keep them occupied by bringing about disagreements among them, and causing them to war among themselves.

The Spaniards arrived at the fort early Feb. 12, took prisoners, plundered supplies and claimed the surrounding area for Spain. The next day they started back for St. Louis. Near the end of the war, Spain used its one-night occupation of Fort St. Joseph in an unsuccessful bid to claim land east of the Mississippi River. From Lawrence Kincaid, "The Spanish Expedition against Fort St. Joseph in 1781, a New Interpretation," Mississippi Valley Historical Review, Vol. 19, No. 2, September, 1932: pages 187-189.

1781 *'The blood flowed in streams'*

Revolutionaries slaughter peace-loving Indians

While the Revolutionary War was raging on the Atlantic coast, Michigan was relatively quiet except as a staging area for British raiding parties supported by Michigan tribes. The British at Detroit were worried about a band of Delaware Indians in Ohio who were living on a Christian mission and had decided to stay out of the conflict. Because of its neutrality, the Moravian mission community was viewed with suspicion by both the British and the Americans at Fort Pitt, Pa. The British brought the Moravian missionaries to Detroit to explain their position at an investigation directed by British Col. Arent Schuyler de Peyster. Missionary David Zeisburger described the inquiry in his diary.

Nov. 9, 1781: We were at last called to the council. Capt. Pipe (a pro-British Indian leader) began his discourse, giving to (de Peyster) his scalps (of rival Indians), which he had brought with him.

The commandant addressed the Indians, saying to them he had had us brought because he had heard complaints against us, especially that we had corresponded with the rebels (Americans) and from time to time given them news when the warriors wished to make attacks on their settlements. If this were so, we were harmful to this government.

(De Peyster questions the missionaries, satisfying himself that the community is not allied with the Americans.)

He then said he was not opposed to the (Delaware) Indians being civilized and instructed in Christianity, but it was pleasing to him; in this matter he would not hinder us, nor interfere in religious matters, but we should be on our guard and not interfere in war matters.

Since he now saw that we had been

Detroit Public Library

David Zeisburger, the missionary summoned to Detroit.

wrongly accused, we could in God's name go back to our Indians and to our families as soon as we pleased.

(The Moravians returned to Ohio, but were told in February 1782 that de Peyster had ordered the missionaries and Indians back to Detroit, where he could keep an eye on them. Zeisburger's diary entry for March 23 describes what happened to Indians gathering corn from storage for the forced march to Detroit.)

The militia, some 200 (Virginians) in number, as we hear, came to Gnadenhutton (Ohio). Our Indians were mostly on the plantations and saw the militia come, but no one thought of fleeing, for they suspected no ill. The militia bade them come into town, telling them no harm would befall them. They trusted and went, but our Indians were all bound, the men being put in one house, the women into another.

Then they began to sing hymns and spoke words of encouragement and consolation one to another until they were all slain. Two well-grown boys, who saw the whole thing and escaped, gave this information. One of these lay under the heaps of slain and was scalped, but finally came to himself and found opportunity to escape. (He) said the blood flowed in streams in the house. They burned the dead bodies, together with the houses.

The American rebels had brained about 90 Indians with mallets. The survivors hurried to Detroit and that summer set up a community with the Moravians on the Clinton River. In 1783, after the Americans had won the Revolutionary War, Zeisburger wrote that he feared for his Moravian-Indian community under American rule. From "The Diary of David Zeisburger," Historical and Philosophical Society of Ohio, 1885: pages 37-81.

Detroit Public Library

Col. Arent Schuyler de Peyster, British commandant at Detroit.

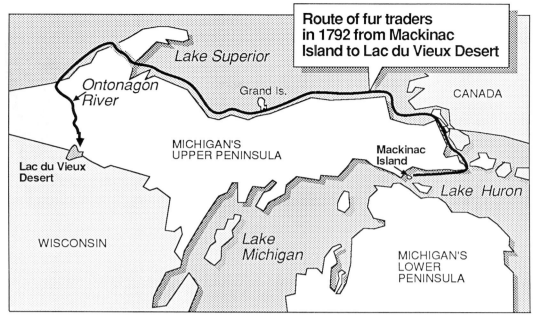

Dominic Trupiano/Detroit Free Press

Jean Baptiste Perrault and his party followed the Ontonagon River and then walked through the woods to Lac du Vieu Desert.

1792 'No one was obliged to enter here'

Animal pelts draw traders deep into the woods

From 1640 to 1840, Michigan furs lured traders, built fortunes and brought nations to war. Though allegiances and alliances changed frequently during those two centuries, the life of the coureur de bois, or woods ranger, seldom varied. Jean Baptiste Perrault wrote a narrative at the urging of Henry Schoolcraft in about 1830. John Sharpless Fox discovered the manuscript among Schoolcraft's papers and speculated, because of the precise

details in the 40-year-old narrative, that Perrault based his account on diaries.

In 1792, on my return from la Pointe Aux Chenes, I remained several days at Mackinac. I resolved to enter (the Ontonagon River). To that end I sold my large canoe and bought two medium canoes. I hired six good men whom I knew well. I gave them good wages, for no one was obliged to enter here, because of the length of the portage. Leaving Mackinac in the middle of July, we arrived (at the river) the third of August, and on the fourth we reached the portage.

I had in the two canoes 40 pieces of merchandise and provisions, which we unloaded at the portage. On the fifth we began to carry. It took us 22 days to reach Pakkwesyawen, where I put *en cache* five kegs of rum, one of powder and two of lead and balls, in order to make better time. We found there old Nez Casse (a Chippewa named Broken Nose) and we went from there to the Lac du Vieu Desert (on the present-day Michigan-Wisconsin border) in 11 days. This made 33 days that we had taken on the portage.

The savages came from all sides (to trade) and at Christmas time I had six packs tied up, five of beaver and one of mixed skins. Le Castor Jaune (a Chippewa named Yellow Beaver) asked for a man to spend the winter with him and look after my credits, and I sent one with him and one with Chonkespa (another Chippewa) as well on the shore of L'Anse (on Lake Superior). During February Chonkespa came to the house with Lefebvre (Pierre Lefebvre, a *coureur de bois* in Perrault's party), the man who had gone to stay with him. The latter was loaded with the dried meat of a large moose, and the savage with a pack of furs, containing 30-plus of all kinds. I gave him one-half keg of rum in payment for what I received and for

what my men would bring. He left well satisfied and said he would come toward sugar time (in spring, when sap begins to run in maple trees and sugar is made).

(In early April) the savages arrived for the last time, when I was poorly paid. They remained in arrears of their credits of more than 300-plus; I got from them the value of 200-plus of all sorts of peltries and one-half pack of beaver, in all. They urged me to return, saying that they would pay me on my return. I told them it was unprofitable; that the portage was too long.

We finished our sugar about the 20th of April, when the snow had disappeared, and I found myself with seven kegs of sugar. (Broken Nose) passed the spring near us, and I hired him to make for me three moose-skin canoes of two skins each, which made each canoe 17 feet long and three feet wide. We descended the river, making 17 short carries — it is one of the worst rivers — and we reached our canoes at the fork without accident.

When I reached Mackinac, beaver, otter, bearskins, marten, (musk)rats, weasels, skunks (were) all at the lowest price.

In the 1830s, Lac du Vieu Desert was used to determine the Michigan-Wisconsin border, which runs through it. From "Michigan Pioneer and Historical Collections," (40 vols., 1877-1929) Vol. 37, Michigan Pioneer and Historical Society, Lansing, 1909 and 1910: pages 508-619.

Fight
for statehood

"We shall probably be allowed to come into the union, if we surrender our rights, but the union of gamblers and pickpockets, to the poor traveler who has just been robbed, is hardly to be desired."
— Lucius Lyon

1791 'Hogs ... running in the streets'

Trouble in small-town Detroit: Missing logs, runaway hogs

Late in the summer of 1791, Detroit and Michigan were part of British-controlled Canada, and the city's population was nearly 500. Most were French, but there were English and Scots, Indians, slaves, free blacks and Americans. These records, from several city departments, show what life was like. The first is a police report sworn out on Aug. 22, 1791.

Complaint on oath of George Setchelstiel, tanner, against Simon Girty, late Indian interpreter:

That on Sunday the 21 of August 1791, being on horseback, he was assaulted by said Simon Girty, who seized his horse by the bridle, making use of abusive words, and after (Setchelstiel) had found means to turn his horse away and get at some distance, said Girty threw two stones at him, the latter of which struck him in the head and gave him a wound from which much blood gushed out, all of which bad treatment he received without having given any provocation prior to having received the wound.

Far more common were offenses such as these, cited two days later in "Violations of Police Regulations":

Mr. Wm. Scott: Two of his cows found in the street. Mr. G. McDougal: Leaving his cart in the street all night. Note well: A number of hogs are daily running in the streets, to the great detriment of the public.

The 1790s even had their own version of potholes. The Aug. 8 "Report on Street Defects" includes a tally of missing logs, with which the city's streets were paved:

The street opposite the church in bad order.

The logs in front of Geo. Leith & Co. in bad order — one missing.

No logs at all before Mr. Hand's house.

The footpath before the major's garden (at the city's main guard post) in bad order.

Fire preparedness was a genuine concern in the wood-and-shingle settlement. But an Aug. 1 report noted that some households and shopkeepers were failing to maintain the required number of ladders, water buckets and bags to carry away goods in the event of fire.

G. McGregor: one bag wanting; Mr. McGregor will have everything.

Rev. Frechet: one bag wanting; one ladder wanting, ready in the course of this week.

N. Williams: one bucket, one bag, one ladder wanting: Mr. N. Williams, having just arrived in town, will have all ready in two days.

Montigny: two ladders wanting; Mr. Montigny has ladders making.

A similar "Report on Defective Chimneys" noted:

Black Diana: Kitchen fireplace wants repairs.

Mrs. Bourbank: chimney in a dangerous condition.

Doctor Holmes: Kitchen chimney wants repairs, one hearth in the upper room in a very dangerous condition.

Wm. Scott: kitchen chimney very bad, the pipe of the stove only 1½ inches from the woodwork.

Despite the vigilance the reports reflect about fire prevention, a blaze in 1805 destroyed or damaged every building in the settlement except one. From Milo M. Quaife, "The John Askin Papers," Vol. 1, Detroit Library Commission, Detroit, 1928: pages 378-395.

Burton Historical Collection, Detroit Public Library

A watercolor of Detroit in 1794 shows what would later be Congress and Jefferson Avenues, a part of the town below, and Fort Lernoult with its defense works.

Library of Congress

William Hull's military career ended with the surrender of Detroit.

Michigan Historical Collections,
University of Michigan

Lewis Cass became governor of the Michigan Territory and later ran for president.

1812 *'Even the women were indignant'*

Two tales of a surrender, two fates for the leaders

The United States was fighting its last war to wrest independence from Britain when, on Aug. 16, 1812, Gen. William Hull, the American commander at Fort Detroit, surrendered the city to approaching British troops without firing a shot. Ten days later, Hull, a Revolutionary War hero and governor of the Michigan Territory, wrote Secretary of War William Eustis to explain why.

At this time, the whole effective force at my disposal at Detroit did not exceed 800 men. Being new troops, and unaccustomed to a camp life, having performed a laborious march; having been engaged in a number of battles and skirmishes in which many had fallen, and more had received wounds; in addition to which a large number being sick, the strength of the Army was thus reduced. The fort at this time was filled with women, and children, and the old and decrepit people of the town and country.

It now became necessary either to fight the enemy in the field, collect the whole force in the fort, or propose terms of capitulation. I could not have carried into the field more than 600 men and left any adequate force in the fort. (Making a stand) must have been attended with a great sacrifice of blood, and no possible advantage for the want of powder and provisions; in addition to this, Cols. (Duncan) McArthur and (Lewis) Cass would have been in a most hazardous situation.

I feared nothing but the last alternative (capitulation). I have dared to adopt it.

(On Sept. 10, one of Hull's colonels, 29-year-old Lewis Cass, wrote to Eustis with his story of the surrender.)

In entering into this capitulation, the general took counsel from his own feelings only. Not an officer was consulted. Not one anticipated a surrender, till he saw the white flag displayed. Even the women were indignant at so shameful a degradation of the American character.

To see the whole of our men flushed with the hope of victory, eagerly awaiting the approaching contest, to see them afterwards dispirited, hopeless and desponding, at least 500 shedding tears because they were not allowed to meet their country's foe and to fight their country's battles, excited sensations which no American has ever before had cause to feel, and which I trust in God will never again be felt, while one man remains to defend the standard of the union.

I was informed by Gen. Hull the morning after the capitulation that the British forces consisted of 1,800 regulars, and that he surrendered to prevent the effusion of human blood. That he magnified their regular force nearly five fold there can be no doubt. Whether the philanthropical reason assigned by him is a sufficient justification for surrendering a fortified town, an Army and a territory is for the government to determine.

President James Madison named Cass to succeed Hull as governor of the Michigan Territory and Hull was court-martialed and sentenced to be shot for cowardice, neglect of duty and conduct unbecoming of an officer. Madison remitted the sentence, citing Hull's previous military career. From "Michigan Pioneer and Historical Collections," (40 vols., 1877-1929) Vol. 40, Michigan Historical Commission, Lansing, 1929: pages 460-485.

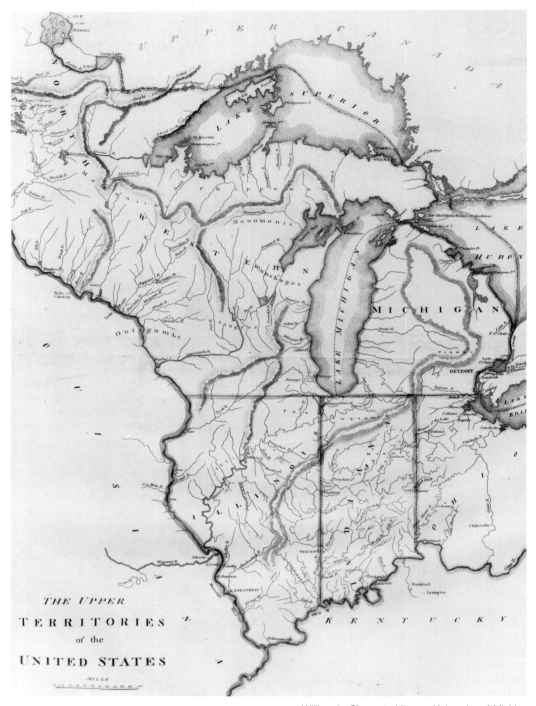

William L. Clements Library, University of Michigan

This map, published at Philadelphia in 1814, shows a low range of mountains in Michigan's Lower Peninsula.

1815 *'Swampy beyond description'*

Surveyors write off Michigan as water-logged wasteland

With a victory in the War of 1812, a young America was eager to reward its soldiers and settle its frontier. Congress ordered that two million acres of the Michigan Territory be surveyed and given to soldiers. Government surveyors looking for potential farmland in southeastern Michigan made their initial reports to Edward Tiffin, surveyor general of the United States. With winter closing in on Nov. 30, 1815, Tiffin sent Congress some strong advice about the land.

The surveyors have been obliged to suspend their operations until the country shall be sufficiently froze so as to bear man and beast. They continued to work, suffering incredible hardships, until today the men and beasts were literally wore down with extreme sufferings and fatigue. The frost set in early, and the ice covered nearly the whole country but broke through at every step, and pack horses could not be got along with them; they were therefore obliged to submit to the climate and its attendant rigors, and desist for a while.

I annex a description of the country which has been sent me and which, I am informed, all the surveyors concur in. The whole of the two million acres appropriated in the Territory of Michigan will not contain anything like one hundred part of that quantity (that) is worth the expense of surveying it. Perhaps it will be proper to make this representation to the president of the United States and he may avert all further proceedings — by directing me to pay off what has been done and abandon the country.

The country is, with some few exceptions, low, wet land, with a very heavy growth of underbrush, intermixed with very bad marshes, but generally very heavily timbered with beech, cottonwood, oak, etc. The streams are generally narrow and very deep compared with their width, the shores and bottoms of which are, with a very few exceptions, swampy beyond description, and it is with difficulty that a place can be found over which horses can be conveyed.

A circumstance peculiar to that country is exhibited in many of the marshes by their being thinly covered with a sward grass, by walking on which evinced the existence of water or a very thin mud immediately under that thin covering, which sinks from six to 18 inches from the pressure of the foot at every step. The margins of many of the lakes and streams are in similar situation, and in many places are literally afloat. On approaching the eastern part of the military lands the country does not contain so many swamps and lakes, but the extreme sterility and barrenness of the soil continues the same. Taking the country altogether so far as has been explored, and with the information received (that) the balance is as bad, there would be not more than one acre in a hundred, if there were one out of a thousand, that would in any case admit of cultivation.

The effect of Tiffin's report on Michigan's development has been disputed, but the immediate result was clear: Although surveying continued, Congress designated land in Illinois and Missouri to pay the veterans. From "Michigan Pioneer and Historical Collections," (40 vols., 1877-1929) Vol. 10, Michigan Pioneer and Historical Society, Lansing, 1908: pages 61-62.

1826 '*A respect for those pioneers*'

Erie Canal opens a flood of settlers to Michigan

In 1826, John Quincy Adams was president of 24 states, and the Erie Canal was less than a year old. The canal, connecting Lake Erie with the Hudson River, had opened a flood of commerce and become a thoroughfare for settlers bound for the Michigan Territory. Thomas McKenney, superintendent of Indian Affairs in Washington, traveled the canal on his way to meet Gov. Lewis Cass and secure a treaty with the Indians. McKenney wrote letters almost every day, describing the canal, horse-drawn stages and the trip across Lake Erie.

June 7

This boat is drawn by three horses, connected to it by means of a rope about 80 feet long. These horses trot along the towpath, as it is called, and which is immediately on the border of the canal, and at the rate, generally, of four miles the hour. The horses are relieved every 10 miles, or 15, when the driver is changed also.

It happened that 40 passengers entered for this trip.

I have lived as much as I could today upon the top of the box, called the deck, and which inclines every way from the middle to let the water off, I suppose, but around which are no railings or net work. But this is done at the risk of being scraped off by the bridges, many of which are so low as to leave scarcely room enough for my body, though I extend it along the deck and spread myself out as flat as a lizard.

June 10

I left Utica at 4 o'clock this morning in the mail stage. We had in the stage — the mail stage — the reasonable, not to say comfortable, number of 14 persons, to say nothing of the driver and the great mail!

June 12

Soon after leaving Rochester, we reached that extraordinary ridge called the Ridge Road. This ridge is in some places but little more than wide enough to allow the passage of the stage. Sometimes it inclines gradually into the valleys on both sides, then again the ways to the depths below are precipitous and appalling!

June 16

I arrived at (Detroit) this morning at 10 o'clock after an agreeable passage from Buffalo of 37 hours, distance about 330 miles. Nothing could be more smooth and beautiful than Lake Erie.

I had noticed, from the time we left Buffalo, a man and his wife, deck passengers — emigrants who owned, in part, the wheels and carts and looms and fixtures for log huts that were soon to be built in the Michigan Territory. He was tall and gaunt and bony, with a long neck, sharp visage, quick movements, long arms and broad hands. She was short, round and not more than half his years. He appeared to be 50 — she not more than five-and-twenty. Around her were hanging three flaxen-headed children, except when every now and then two of them — the third was too small for such exercise — would race it around the deck or tumble over some of the baggage — but happy as happy could be. The father partook of the pleasure of these little ones, but the mother was pensive. I noticed that her eyes were often filled with tears! I did not see her smile once during the voyage — but noticed that she often sighed. This never failed to afflict her husband, who would sit by her and take her hand.

I have a great respect for those pioneers — they are the fathers and mothers who are

34

New York Historical Society

There was little room between the tops of the canal boats and the many bridges under which they passed.

destined to provide the country with many a noble defender, and whose arms, well practiced by the use of the ax and the plow, and the eyes, with catching a ready sight down the barrels of their rifles, will, in time of need, be found as they have been found, foremost in danger and efficient and victorious in the battle.

From Thomas L. McKenney, "Sketches of a Tour to the Lakes, of the Character and Customs of the Chippeway Indians, and of Incidents Connected with the Treaty of Fond du Lac": pages 48-107. Originally published in Baltimore in 1827, it was reprinted by Ross & Haines, Inc., Minneapolis, Minn., in 1959.

1827 'This might be a healthy place'

Visitor from Pennsylvania sees room for growth

Salmon Keeney, a fifth-generation American, came from Pennsylvania to examine firsthand the stories he had heard of the Michigan Territory. He arrived in Detroit in 1827, the first year a steamboat was built there, the year sidewalks — usually made of wood — first were required and when the city's water was supplied by a pump house on the wharf. Keeney wrote his observations in a three-by-six-inch diary.

July 5

Arrive at Detroit City at 1 a.m. This city is about 20 miles from Lake Erie on the bank of Detroit River. I have been five days and six nights coming from Buffalo in the steamboat Enterprise. The accommodations are bad, hands and fireman are all masters but none can command honor; fighting, quarreling, and discord.

July 7

Detroit city is in full view of the Canada shore, about two miles across the river. The ground is sandy and dry, suitable for the building of a city, sufficiently high to have the water drain off each way. The vast square of block houses, which enclosed about two acres, is going to decay and the pickets (fences) falling down. Here (Gen. William) Hull surrendered his Army (to the British). I should think from appearances that this might be a healthy place and a place of considerable business, though like every other place along the lake there is too much competition for the benefit of the mercantile part of the community.

July 8

I start from Detroit on horseback and take the road to Ann Arbor, which leads along the River Rouge, a small, sluggish stream.

We arrive at Ann Arbor at 6 p.m., 40 miles from Detroit. This is the county seat of Washtenaw County. This is situated on the River Huron, a small stream on which are erected mills, and is sufficiently large for that purpose on a limited scale. The land is oak openings and the town is laid into too small lots for so inland a place, and held at the most extravagant prices. There is some good timbered land in the neighborhood, but this is the poorest part of Michigan I have seen. The people proud and distant; poor accommodations at the taverns.

July 9

We take the road to Monroe and arrive there at 3 p.m. On this route we pass through a timbered country and the best land I ever saw in any country, but generally lies low. We pass on this route the great prairie, which is supposed to contain about 4,000 acres; is low and wet, but in places produces fine grass. We have passed many others but none so large and we sometimes have seen the deer bounding through the grass for miles.

July 21

I go to the Bay Settlement (Erie) and settle my timber business with the French; agree with Cornwell to see to my land in that place and prevent the French from cutting timber there.

July 22

Monroe is the capital of a county of the same name situated on the south bank of the Raisin River, four miles from its confluence with Lake Erie. Its water privileges are the best of any I have seen in the territory and will admit of any number of mills. It is a neat little town and though in a state of infancy must in a few years become a place of business. There is four drygoods stores, two taverns, one courthouse, a number of

Courtesy Mary J. Fitch Mihovich

Salmon Keeney about 1847

grocery and mechanics of various and useful occupations, two schools, a polite and hospitable society. Here are to be seen the natives of the forest in vast numbers every day going to and coming from Malden, where the bureau from the British government (makes) presents of goods as a reward for their services against the United States during the last war. Will the United States suffer this!!

The next year, Keeney moved his family to Monroe County. He is regarded as founder of the first English speaking school in Erie Township and was the area's second postmaster. He is credited with changing its name from Bay Settlement to Erie. He died in Erie on March 9, 1847. From a diary submitted by Keeney's great-great-great granddaughter, Mary J. Fitch Mihovich of Oak Park.

Michigan Historical Commission

Fort Gratiot, as seen from the northwest

1832 *'Swept off by the disease'*

Cholera-stricken soldiers touch off an epidemic

In 1832, the Michigan Territory became host to a deadly newcomer. On July 4, a ship carrying soldiers to Chicago to fight Black Hawk's uprising tied up at Detroit and some soldiers were taken ashore with cholera. By morning, 11 were dead. The ship was sent away, but the city had already been infected. Within days, another transport infected Ft. Gratiot, at the present site of Port Huron. Scared soldiers deserted, trying to escape the disease, but spreading it instead. These letters describe the pestilence.

Fort Gratiot, July 10

There has been only one new case of cholera among the troops during the last 24 hours. There now remain 13 or 14 cases, of which it is believed two-thirds will recover.

The dead bodies of the deserters are literally strewed along the road between here and Detroit. No one dares give them relief, not even a cup of water. A person on his way here from Detroit passed six lying groaning with the agonies of the cholera under one tree, and saw one corpse by the roadside, half eaten up by the hogs.

There are three or four companies of soldiers about 15 miles below who also have this dreadful disease among them.

Detroit, July 12

The cholera continues to prevail in this city. Between 30 and 40 cases, in all, have occurred; and of these about 18 have resulted in death. Most of the others are convalescent; the remainder doubtful. The town is almost deserted by its laboring inhabitants; and the countenances of the remaining citizens, with some few exceptions, exhibit marks of unusual depression and melancholy. This is greatly to be lamented. The effect is unhappy.

I regret to add that the intelligence from the regular troops is disastrous. Of the three companies of artillery under Col. Twiggs, and two or three more companies of infantry with them, few remain. These troops, you will recollect, landed from the steamboat Henry Clay below Fort Gratiot. A great number of them have been swept off by the disease. Nearly all the others have deserted. Of the deserters, scattered all over the country, some have died in the woods and their bodies have been devoured by the wolves. Others have taken their flight to the world of the spirits without a companion to close their eyes or console the last moments of their existence. Their straggling survivors are occasionally seen marching, some of them know not whither, with their knapsacks on their backs, shunned by the terrified inhabitants as the source of mortal pestilence.

Detroit, July 13

The cholera has essentially abated in this city. No new cases have occurred within the last 24 hours. One or two deaths, from previous cases, have occurred. Several have recovered and the remainder appear to be convalescing.

From the encampment of the remnant of regular troops near Fort Gratiot, information has today been received. The disease is disappearing there also.

In two weeks, 58 Detroiters contracted cholera and 28 died, including Elizabeth Cass, 21-year-old daughter of Secretary of War Lewis Cass. In Marshall, 18 of the city's 70 residents were stricken and eight of them died. These excerpts are from letters reprinted in the July 15, 1897, issue of the Port Huron Weekly Times.

1833 *'We live upon the fat of the land'*

Two bedrooms, 11 glass windows make for a frontier palace

In 1831, Martha L. White's sons Enoch and Jonathon left South Hadley, Mass., to build a new family home in Michigan. Enoch had just brought the 50-year-old widow and her other six children along the Erie Canal, across Lake Erie and through Michigan to their log cabin on the banks of the Flint River in Lapeer. On June 9, 1833, she described the trip in a letter to a friend, Margaret McMasters.

After the elapse of 15 days we have arrived at our place of destination in Michigan. We did not leave Albany until Monday, when we took the line boat bound for Buffalo and found good company and several from Massachusetts, Vermont and Connecticut, most of whom were on their way to Michigan. From the first of May last to the 17th, seven steamboats landed at Detroit from Buffalo with 2,610 passengers and now you can judge for yourself whether you think Michigan will be settled soon or not.

We passed by many neat and beautiful villages and among them were Troy (N.Y.) and Little Falls (N.Y.). For three miles the canal is formed by throwing up a wall into the river 20 or 30 feet and this is said to be the most expensive part of the canal. A beautiful marble aqueduct crosses the river at this place and loads into the basin opposite where boats discharge and receive lading.

Passengers that are disposed to view the place generally leave the boat at the first lock and walk until they reach the last, which are six in number, by which the boat is so much detained that a person may walk quite leisurely through the most wild and romantic scenery imaginable.

Syracuse is the most important place between Utica and Rochester. It contains 900 buildings, among which are two extensive hotels on each side of the canal.

Rochester (N.Y.) is the most extensive village in the western part of the state. It contains 2,000 buildings and a population of 13,000.

The boat left Rochester about 11 in the morning and arrived at Buffalo Tuesday, where we found the steamboat (Enterprise) ready to sail for Detroit.

Jonathon was on shore to receive us and accompanied us to the Mansion House. After dinner we started for Lapeer and reached Pontiac the first day. Rose early the next morning, renewed our journey. About noon it began to rain quite hard but we were obliged to keep on, as there were no houses on the road. Saturday about 5 o'clock we were in sight of our log house which is 60 feet long. It contains a kitchen, parlor, with a good floor and is sealed up like any house. It also contains two good bedrooms, a parlor chamber and a kitchen chamber and it has 11 glass windows like any palace. Should you chance to peep in you would find us all contented and not any of us have been homesick since we came. Austin (the youngest child) would not come back for anything. The goods all came perfectly safe and not anything was broken with the exception of a blue platter which was split in the middle. We have all good things here, one barrel of molasses, 1½ of sugar, and so you see we live upon the fat of the land. As for Indians, snakes, mosquitoes and rats, I have seen none, and flies are not an inhabitant of this region.

Martha L. White died in Lapeer at age 63 on May 12, 1847. This letter was submitted by great-great-grandson Enoch White of St. Johns. A former newspaper editor and publisher, he is known as Ink White.

Detroit Institute of Arts

Steamers jammed the Detroit waterfront in this 1837 painting by William J. Bennett.

1834 *'We must . . . demand admission'*

Abolitionist anticipates roads, the train and statehood

An abolitionist in her late 20s, Elizabeth Margaret Chandler had come with her family from Philadelphia to "Hazelbank," their new farm near Adrian. In letters to an aunt back home, she described her new life in the Michigan Territory, which in 1834 included all of Iowa, Minnesota, Wisconsin and parts of the Dakotas.

There has been much talk here lately about constructing a railroad through the territory. It would be a great advantage to the inland farmers, and the country generally favors the undertaking very much, as it will not be so expensive as over a broken and irregular surface. If constructed it will pass through Adrian, I suppose.

Brother has been for a couple of days past working on the roads. They are building another bridge across the river. Our new country requires the formation and laying out of many roads.

As to our being engaged with building and work people; do not give thyself a moment's concern. These frame barns and buildings do not require so much work and so many laborers as the substantial stone ones of Pennsylvania.

Brother has engaged some young apple trees and grafts wherewith to set us out a small orchard this spring, which, though anxious for it, he has not been able to do before, so that you must not expect us to treat you with apple dumplings and cider when you come to see us, though as to the latter we are such temperate folks here that I do not know that there will be any presses erected even when fruit is plenty.

Anti-slavery principles, too, are gaining ground. Daniel Smith mentioned the subject in his sermon, and spoke upon it for some time. Thee may suppose I listened to him with much pleasure.

Another census of the population of Michigan will probably be taken next summer, as it is thought that the southern members of Congress will object to our territory being received into the union unless a slave state could be admitted at the same time, so we must be able to demand admission with a population of 60,000 inhabitants.

We had a barn raising several weeks ago. It went up snugly and safely. There was a large number of hands, between 40 and 50 altogether, and if thee had happened to step in on the afternoon or morning before the raising, thee would have found Aunt Ruth and me quite deeply immersed in preparation of pies, puddings and cakes, such being the articles provided for refreshments. We had intended putting our tables out of doors, but the afternoon was rather cool and dusty, so that we were obliged to spread them within, not for the men to sit down to, for that would have been out of the question, but to cluster around as well as they were able or to obtain their supplies, retreat to another part of the room and give place to others. So much for a "raising" in the "back woods."

The Erie & Kalamazoo Railroad reached Adrian from Toledo in 1836 and, in 1837, Michigan became a state. Elizabeth Chandler never wrote about those events, though. She was ill when she wrote these letters and died not long after the barn raising. From the Elizabeth Chandler papers, box two, in the Michigan Historical Collections at the University of Michigan's Bentley Historical Library.

From "The Political Works of Elizabeth Margaret Chandler"

Elizabeth Margaret Chandler, a Quaker, oganized Michigan's first anti-slavery society.

1836 *'To bung Ohio's eyes'*

Wolverines go to war to hang onto Toledo

In the mid-1830s, the Michigan Territory and the State of Ohio were at war over a narrow strip of land at their shared border. The strip included Toledo, and each side wanted its port on Lake Erie. Although there were militias, invasions and prisoners of war, the Toledo War was not fought on a grand scale. The lone casualty was a stab wound. In 1836, it was clear that the dispute would not be settled on the field of battle but in the halls of Congress, where Ohio, as a state, had the clear upper hand. It looked as if Michigan would have to settle for a cold expanse of virtually uninhabited land — the western two-thirds of the Upper Peninsula. Michiganders sang of their discontent and the exploits of Territorial Gov. Stevens T. Mason, Ohio Gov. Robert Lucas and Michigan Brig. Gen. Joseph Brown in the "Toledo War Song."

Come, all ye Michiganians, and lend a hearing ear;
Remember, for Toledo we once took up sword and spear.
And now, to give that struggle o'er and trade away that land,
I think it's not becoming of valiant-hearted men.

In eighteen hundred thirty-five there was a dreadful strife
Betwixt Ohio and this State; they talked of taking life.
Ohio claimed Toledo and so did Michigan;
They both declared they'd have it, with its adjoining land.

Old Lucas gave his order for all to hold a court;
And Stevens Thomas Mason, he thought he'd have some sport.

He called upon the Wolverines and asked them for to go
To meet this rebel Lucas, his court to overthrow.

We held a general muster; we trained till past sundown.
At the head of all the Wolverines marched Mason and old Brown,
A valiant-hearted general, a governor likewise,
A set of jovial Wolverines to bung Ohio's eyes.

When we got down to Toledo, old Lucas was not there;
He had heard that we were coming and ran away with fear.
To hear the wolves a-howling scared the poor devil so,
He said, before he'd fight them, he'd give up Toledo.

Mark the republic spirit that they have now displayed;
At first they'd have Toledo or lose their lives in aid;
But now the song they sing to us is: "Trade away that land
For that poor, frozen country beyond Lake Michigan."

They say that we must surely trade, or we shall be cast out;
That we shall lose our five percent as sure as we do not;
That we can't be admitted into the bold Union,
But that we must, like the fifth calf, stand back and just look on.

44

Detroit Institute of Arts

A humorous painting of Michigan's 1837 election shows Gov. Stevens T. Mason paying a dollar for a vote and a horseman waving a Mason banner. In the background, an American flag flies from a liberty pole.

The "five percent" refers to money states received from the sale of federal lands within their borders. Michigan accepted the compromise on Dec. 14 at the Frostbitten Convention in Ann Arbor and was admitted to the union. From "Michigan Pioneer and Historical Collections," (40 vols., 1877-1929) Vol. 6, Michigan Pioneer and Historical Society, Lansing, 1884: pages 60-61.

1836 'Gamblers and pickpockets'

An embittered Michigan loses Toledo, gains much of the Upper Peninsula

Lucius Lyon, one of Michigan's first two senators, was pressing for statehood in 1836 while fighting to hang onto the Toledo strip along the Michigan-Ohio border. It was becoming clear to him that if Michigan was to enter the union, it would have to drop its claim to the triangular piece of land. The resolution of the conflict unfolds in his letters, written in Washington in 1836 and sent to various constituents.

Jan. 3

There is very strong probability that both houses will pass a bill for cutting off from Michigan and giving to Ohio all she asks. This they will probably do before acting on our application for admission as a state. Then when it shall be proposed to us to change our constitution so as to conform to the new boundary, the question will arise, shall we do so? I say, for one, we shall never acknowledge the power of Congress to take from us the tract claimed by Ohio. It is enough to submit to the unconstitutional action of that body in giving part of our territory in Indiana — more than this we cannot bear, especially as there cannot be found in either house a single member, except from the states interested, who will say that state has any legal claim. (The Northwest Ordinance had proposed that Michigan's southern boundary be a line due east from the southern tip of Lake Michigan. When Indiana entered the union, it included land north of that line, giving it access to lake Michigan and taking land that some considered to be Michigan's.)

Feb. 4

I have no doubt the committee will be willing to give us all the country west of Lake Michigan and north and east of the Menominee River of Green Bay and the

Michigan boundaries and the Toledo strip

CANADA
MICHIGAN
WISCONSIN
Western boundary
MICHIGAN
Michigan-Indiana boundary 1816
Boundary claimed by Ohio
Toledo
ILLINOIS
Boundary claimed by Michigan until 1816
Claimed by Michigan until 1837
Disputed area
INDIANA
OHIO

Dominic Trupiano / Detroit Free Press

Michigan lost territory on lakes Michigan and Erie in border fights with Indiana and Ohio, but gained most of the Upper Peninsula.

Montreal River of Lake Superior, thus giving us the greater part of the coast of that lake, which may at some future time be valuable. (This is the western boundary of

Michigan Historical Collections,
University of Michigan

Lucius Lyon was about 50 when this portrait was made in 1850.

Michigan's Upper Peninsula.) This seems to be the division fixed on in case our southern boundary should be broken up, which I yet hope will not be done.

Feb. 18

The corruption and management of the delegation in Congress from Ohio and Indiana is about to deprive Michigan of the country claimed by (Ohio), and to compensate us in some measure, the committee will probably give us a strip of country along the southern shore of Lake Superior, where we can raise our own Indians in all time to come and supply ourselves now and then with a little bear meat for delicacy.

March 12

All parties are courting the electoral votes of Ohio, Indiana and Illinois and poor Michigan must be sacrificed. We shall probably be allowed to come into the union, if we surrender our rights, but the union of gamblers and pickpockets, to the poor traveler who has just been robbed, is hardly to be desired.

March 23

I perceive that some of the Michigan people are opposed to receiving any addition to our state on the northwest because they view it as an exchange for the tract claimed by Ohio. If this were the case I should be opposed to it myself. But it is not so. We have lost the tract claimed by Ohio. The only question that remains is, shall we not endeavor, as our boundaries are broken up, to get now an addition on the northwest which may in some future time become valuable?

April 3

The bill for the admission of Michigan has passed the Senate and is expected to be taken up in the House and passed there in a week or two. The conditions of our admission are that the boundaries proposed for our state by Congress shall receive the assent of a convention of delegates elected by the people and that thereupon the president shall issue his proclamation declaring Michigan a State of the Union. Humiliating as these terms are, they are the best that can possibly be obtained.

The compromise cost Michigan 468 square miles of land, Toledo, and the harbor there. To the north, Michigan gained about 13,000 square miles of land and hundreds of miles of coastline on lakes Michigan and Superior. Within a dozen years, the area would become the nation's largest producer of copper and, a few decades later, the nation's leader in iron ore. From "Michigan Pioneer and Historical Collections," (40 vols., 1877-1929) Vol. 27, Michigan Pioneer and Historical Society, Lansing, 1897: pages 470-494.

1838 'Many hardships and privation'

State's future capital is just a village in the wilderness

A financial crash sent a tide of settlers and speculators rippling across the country during the Panic of 1837. One of them was John Child, who described the 17-month-old state of Michigan in a letter to his sister, Janette, in Tompkins County, N.Y.

Detroit, July 1, 1838

My Dear Sister:

You will, I doubt not, be surprised at receiving a letter from me, especially as it bears date from the capital of Michigan. You are aware that for a long time, I have had a curiosity and an inclination to visit this state; as I was out of business, that curiosity I determined to gratify and left Seneca Falls (N.Y.) some five weeks since for the western world.

Of course, you have learned that Father left Penn Yan (N.Y.) about the first day of May for this state. I have been into the interior about 100 miles, to Ingham County, and stayed several days with Father. He has quite a valuable lot, but it is heavy timbered and will require a great deal of labor to improve it. There is a village laid out within a mile of his lot; it at present consists of some half-a-dozen log dwellings and some 20 or 30 inhabitants; and bids fair to be a village of some considerable importance; but now it is literally in the wilderness. It will probably be the seat of Ingham County.

With some parts of the country through which I passed, I was much pleased. The state undoubtedly possesses, on the whole, a very rich soil and a great many natural advantages. She is rapidly progressing in improvements and will in the course of a few years be a rich and populous state. Detroit is much more of a respectable-looking place and larger withal than I expected to find (and) there is not so many French and

Burton Historical Collection, Detroit Public Library

Michigan's first capitol was in Detroit. It finished its years as a school building.

foreigners as I had supposed: Most of the businessmen, and a large portion of the inhabitants, are from eastern states, more particularly from New York; and as a general thing it (is) so throughout the state.

Those who move into the interior undergo a great many hardships and privation. The only object I can see for the people of the east coming here, the farmers more particularly, is the low price of land. The soil throughout our wide and extended country must and will be valuable. A person owning a small lot only, in almost any part of it, can get a good livelihood, and live, as it were, independent, from cultivating it.

Everything in the provision and clothing bears an enormous price, more so in the interior of the state, which I should think comes very hard upon new immigrants. Still, they are daily pouring into the state.

Detroit was Michigan's capital until 1847, when a capitol was built at Lansing in the wilderness Child visited — Ingham County. From a letter submitted by Jessie Mae Sanderson of Livonia, whose husband, C. Gordon, is the great-grandson of John Child's sister Harriet, who came to Michigan with her father.

Growing pains

"We have eight head of cattle and four sheep and market for everything we have to spare but hard times for money."
— Nancy Hovey Newell

1839 'A pack of shavers and robbers'

Travel tips: Brings beds, spoons and the irons from the planes

John Lathers, one of eight children, came to Michigan from Cootehill, County Cavan, Ireland. On Feb. 10, 1839, having recently learned that his parents had died, he wrote to his brothers and sisters from Nankin, in Wayne County, to tell them how to make the trip to America.

If you are all coming out it will be necessary for you to fetch your beds and bedclothes with you and also some cooking utensils, and fetch any clothes that are worth wearing. You should fetch as much coarse wearing clothes as you think will be sufficient to do you for two or three years, for they cost more than twice as much here, hats or shoes excepted.

Fetch any good books you have with you, except such as are very large. If you have any knives or forks or silver spoons or such small articles as are not much weight, you may as well fetch them with you, for all such things are carried here by merchants from England and sold at a most enormous profit.

I think it would be well for you to fetch a few of the best of the tools that are in the workshop if there are any of them there yet, gimlets and such like. Also take the irons out of the planes, one and all, and fetch them with you. And if there is any good hammer, fetch them. All such things can be got here but it is probable you will get very little for them there.

Take notice when you go to Liverpool you will find runners in all places inviting you to take your passage and lodging and so on.

But give no heed to any of them for they are one and all a pack of shavers and robbers. And when you leave home, do not let your mind be known to everyone you meet with. Whatever money you have when you are leaving home, you should either have it sewed in a belt or in some part of your clothes which you would always keep on.

Courtesy Thomas Girdwood Macfie

John Lathers was one of the first white settlers in the area that is now Garden City. He was married in 1840 and lived until 1905.

When you come to New York, do not throw away any of your cooking utensils or provisions as is commonly done, for you can use them on the way here.

When you get to Albany, take passage on the Western Canal for Buffalo and be careful that they do not charge you an over-price. The regular price is 1½ cents per mile; the distance is 363 miles. When you get to Buffalo (on Lake Erie) take your passage on the steamboat for Detroit. When you come to Detroit, get your baggage on the railroad cars for Dearborn.

When in Dearborn, you must look for some safe place to leave anything you have with you until you come and look for us. When you leave Dearborn, go four miles west on the Chicago Turnpike, where you will find a large house painted red, standing on the right-hand side of the road, occupied as a tavern and known by the name of Ruff's Tavern. Pass that a very short distance and you will find a road turning to the right hand; (go two) miles and you will be where we live.

Lathers lived in the area that is Garden City today. His descendants and those of his brothers and sisters are now scattered from Maryland to Alaska to Hawaii. From a letter submitted by Lathers' great-grandson, Thomas Girdwood Macfie, of Royal Oak.

Cass County Historical Commission

Niles, as depicted in "Map of the Counties Cass, Van Buren and Berrien, Michigan, 1860."

1840 'Notorious even in the West'

Missionary fights infidels, reclaims backsliders in the wicked town of Niles

In 1840, the United States had a population of 17 million, the national debt was 21 cents per person and the Rev. J.N. Parsons was preaching in Niles. An American Home Missionary Society minister, he wrote regular reports on his work to his superiors in New England. These excerpts from two January letters describe his efforts to find converts in "notorious" Niles and his need for continued assistance.

The time has come for me to render you an account of my operations for the first quarter under your commission, and you will probably be surprised to hear from me in Michigan. The reason is, when I arrived here, the roads had become almost impassable, my family and horse worn out and navigation on Lake Michigan suspended.

Niles is a village of 1,100 or 1,200 inhabitants — about 25 miles from the mouth of St. Joseph in Lake Michigan, surrounded by a most beautiful country of openings and prairies. The settlement was commenced seven or eight years ago and it has been notorious even at the West for wickedness. The stores were all open on the Sabbath and that was the great business day. The minister who formed the church five years ago told me that once when he was preaching on the *Sabbath* at the sound of a flatboat horn coming down the river, all his male hearers but one left the house to see it. Since that time many pious families have moved in and a church was gathered.

There have been a few thrilling incidents, one or two of which I will relate.

One of the two first converts had just finished and carpeted a room over his store for a club room, where he might get his comrades together, smoke, drink wine and be jolly — when God met him and he went to that room — got on his knees and dedicated himself and it to God. It is used since as a place of prayer for the converts and a place of retirement for Christians to labor and pray with sinners.

Day before yesterday, a young merchant, who had opposed the revival and hated me for breaking up a Christmas sleigh ride, heard that his little brother prayed at my house the night before, broke down and gave up to the spirit.

The son of one of our members, a lad of 15 or 16, was accustomed to go to the mill last summer and contend for the Bible with the infidels. He attended our sacrament two weeks ago and was awakened, went home (and told) one of the worst of them: "You poisoned my mind last summer with your arguing and made me doubt the truth of the Bible, and now I am lost and you have ruined my soul!" The infidel was so overwhelmed with his guilt that he came to the village — got laudanum (opium) — met the boy as he returned — shook hands with him, besought his pardon — went to the mill and swallowed the poison. He was suspected and charged but replied, "It isn't in the power of God or the devil to prevent my dying now" — a cathartic was given and his life saved. He now attends (church), and is anxious, if not "in his right mind."

One most interesting part of my labor, and fruit of the work, I have not mentioned. It is the reclaiming of backsliders. Men who have come from your (New England) churches left their religion behind or buried it in our forests. One man keeps a groggery inn, sends his children to dancing school — yet has a *conscience*. Oh, brother, you cannot *feel* the blessedness of missionary work.

From a book of missionary letters collected by Maurice F. Cole (ed.), "Voices from the Wilderness," Edwards Brothers, Inc., Ann Arbor, 1961: pages 207-213.

1840 *'Hard times for money'*

Yankees scratch out a living from Michigan's soil

Michigan farm families, many from New York and New England, were struggling in 1840 to put down roots in an economy that had been ravaged by short-term speculation and "wildcat" banks that printed money with little or no gold to back it up. Nancy Hovey Newell, in her late 20s, and her 34-year-old husband, William, described their farm in southeastern Michigan in a September letter to William's sisters in western New York.

Dear Sisters,

We are living on a farm about nine miles west of Adrian, a half-mile from the public road. It will be four years this month since we came on our farm. There was 10 acres cleared. Now we have 33 acres (in) improvement and 13 mostly logged, which has been done this summer and which he (William) intends to sow with wheat this fall if possible. We have raised five acres of hay, which will probably yield about 100 bushels, (and) three acres of corn. He cut about eight acres of hay. We have eight head of cattle and four sheep and market for everything we have to spare but hard times for money. A living stream of water (is) running through the place and sugar orchard, so we make our own sugar and some to spare. We live in a log house and have a frame barn. This year we made over 100 yards of cloth. Our society is tolerably good, though not so refined as in olden places. More Methodist people than any other denomination here. They hold meetings every Sabbath at the schoolhouse a half-mile from us.

William talks of visiting you this fall if he can get his work done in season. Says he would like to have you look out for three bushels of dried apples and half a bushel of dried peaches if you can get them for Michigan money.

I expect that William will finish this

Courtesy Elizabeth Newell Kurtz

William Newell died in 1853, leaving his wife, Nancy, with five children between the ages of 7 and 17.

letter and I must close by requesting you to write soon and often.

Dear Sisters,

You may think there is no need of any more after you have seen Nancy's epistle. She states that I intend to visit you this fall, but you must not make your eyes sore alooking after me. Indeed you would not if you knew how much I have to do before I can come, but providence permitting I shall try to make you a visit this fall. It is more healthy here this summer than last. Crops very good but reduced to a very low rate.

I find that we have to carry a steady hand to get along and come out even at the year's end with the present reduced prices, but we have been blessed with good health in a tolerable good degree, and the hard times found me almost clear of debt.

My eyes are agrowing heavy by working in the smoke through the day, and I must draw to a close.

Six generations of the Newell family were born and reared on that farm. Elizabeth Newell Kurtz of Onsted, who submitted this letter, said her family made maple syrup from the trees in the farm's sugar orchard until the 1950s and raised sheep on the farm until it was sold in 1982.

1844 'I am not property now'

Underground Railroad leads to a new state, a new life

After an odyssey of escape, recapture and another escape from slavery, Henry Bibb was finally free, planning the day he could bring his wife and daughter to freedom on the Underground Railroad. William Gatewood, the Kentucky slaveholder from whom Bibb escaped, had just learned that Bibb was in Detroit and had written to him. On March 23, 1844, Bibb wrote this response.

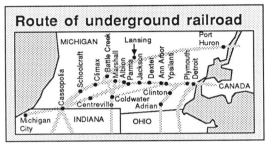

Dominic Trupiano/Detroit Free Press

Thousands of slaves followed the Underground Railroad through southern Michigan.

Dear Sir:

I am happy to inform you that you are not mistaken in (that I am) the man whom you sold as property and received pay for as such. But I thank God that I am not property now, but am regarded as a man like yourself, and although I live far north, I am enjoying a comfortable living by my own industry. If you should ever chance to be traveling this way and will call on me, I will use you better than you did me while you held me as a slave. Think not that I have any malice against you for the cruel treatment which you inflicted on me while I was in your power. As it was the custom of your country to treat your fellow men as you did me and my family, I can freely forgive you.

I wish to be remembered in love to my aged mother and friends; please tell her that if we should never meet again in this life, my prayer shall be to God that we may meet in heaven, where parting shall be no more.

You may perhaps think hard of us for running away from slavery, but as to myself, I have but one apology to make for it, which is: I have only to regret that I did not start at an earlier period. I might have been free long before I was. But you had it in your power to have kept me there much longer than you did. I think it is very probable that I should have been a toiling slave on your property today, if you had treated me differently.

To be compelled to stand by and see you whip and slash my wife without mercy, when I could afford her no protection, not even by offering myself to suffer the lash in her place, was more than I felt it to be the duty of a slave husband to endure, while the way was open to Canada. My infant child was also frequently flogged by Mrs. Gatewood for crying, until its skin was bruised literally purple. This kind of treatment was what drove me from home and family, to seek a better home for them. But I am willing to forget the past. I should be pleased to hear from you again, on the reception of this, and should also be very happy to correspond with you often, if it should be agreeable to yourself. I subscribe myself a friend to the oppressed, and Liberty forever.

The next year, 1845, Bibb risked recapture and returned to Kentucky for his wife, Malinda, and their daughter, Frances. Upon learning that his wife and her master were living together, he gave up, returned to Michigan and threw his energies into rallying Northerners against slavery. This letter was reprinted in "Narrative of the Life and Adventures of Henry Bibb, an American Slave," published by the author in New York in 1849.

Courtesy Barbara Spalding Ely

William P. Spalding stands in front of the store he operated at the Soo with Charles C. Child in the 1850s.

<u>1847</u> *'Snowshoes dug away the snow'*

Soo merchant's shopping trip by sled, train and ferry

In February 1847, William P. Spalding, a 24-year-old shopkeeper in Sault Ste. Marie, set out for New York to arrange his spring shipment. There were no cars, few trains, and the Mackinac Bridge would not be built for more than a century, so Spalding walked the first 250 miles or so on snowshoes. Years later, he told his story.

I concluded to do what others did and get my goods earlier than others that waited for opening of navigation, so I started, accompanied by a man by the name of Converse with two men and train of two dogs for Mackinac Island.

The first day we walked about 10 miles, the voyageurs ahead followed by the dog

55

train making a fair trail, for Converse and myself were tired enough as we were tender and soft. Having reached a maple ridge where water was found in a stream, we made camp. Converse and myself with our snowshoes dug away the snow to the earth, making a place, say, 10 feet square. The men cut wood and made a fire. We were made quite comfortable and ready for supper, which was pork, hard bread and tea. After a smoke, we wrapped ourselves in our blankets and laid down to rest and sleep. From our fatigue we dropped off at once, but the cold awoke us after an hour or two and we arose to warm up and again try to sleep. In the morning early after drying our mitts and moccasins, eating breakfast, packing (we) made good progress.

Third day across the straits to Mackinac Island, where we were welcomed heartily by acquaintances and invited to a ball that night. We was young and could not resist the temptation to meet the belles of the island.

In the morning we found the straits had frozen over to Bois Blanc Island. We packed up and left, walking over on the ice to south side Bois Blanc. The next morning across to mainland.

From Tawas to Point Au Gres we had the worst storm of snow and high northwest wind yet encountered and glad to reach the lighthouse, where we were fed with lake trout and potatoes, which after salt pork and hardtack for so many days we ate voraciously. Trout is very poor food for pedestrians. Next day we made only 10 miles to Pine River.

(Leaving Saginaw two days later, the travelers went by sled to Flint) where we got a train to Pontiac and from there on railroads to Detroit. From Detroit went across river to Windsor and took stage via Chatham, London, Hamilton and Niagara Falls and Buffalo, thence on four railroads to Albany, boat to New York, and my trip was finished.

William Spalding died in 1913 at the age of 92. He had three sons and Barbara Spalding Ely of Birmingham, daughter of his youngest son, submitted this account.

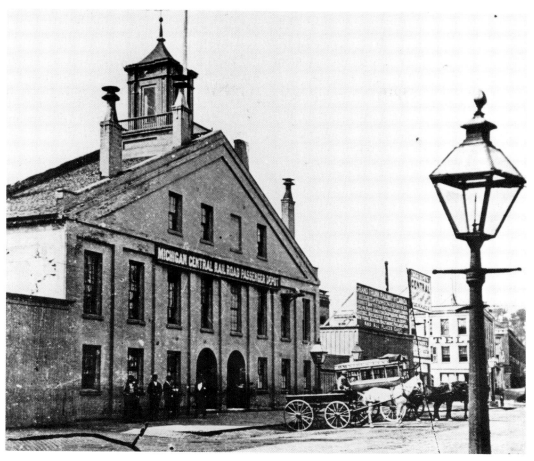

Burton Historical Collection, Detroit Public Library

The Michigan Central Railroad passenger depot in 1848.

<u>1851</u> *'Locked up in a gloomy prison'*

Railroad rebels of Jackson go on trial in Detroit

Farmers in southern Michigan felt as if they had been run over by the arrival of the railroads. Fences were cut, rails were laid across fields and livestock frequently was killed by trains. Farmers derailed the iron interlopers, shot at them and stoned them. The fight reached a fiery climax with the burning of the Michigan Central Railroad freight depot in Detroit. After the blaze was declared arson, about 40 men in south-central Michigan were arrested and brought — by train — to Detroit. Charged with arson and conspiracy, they went through a widely publicized trial with Sen.

57

William H. Seward of New York as defense attorney. One prisoner was Abel F. Fitch of Jackson County, leader of the ragtag revolt. He wrote these letters to his wife, Amanda, from his jail cell.

April 21, 1851

This is the first time I ever addressed you from such a place and I hope to God it will be the last. Arriving in Detroit about 5 p.m., we were then taken and marched to the jail, each accompanied by an officer two by two. I being a captain, they placed me in front, of course, and we gave the Detroit folks a good opportunity to take a fair view of us. We looked like a Connecticut general training and must have been a great satisfaction to the R.R. folks.

April 22

The R.R. folks think they have got us completely in their clutches and feel disposed to wrong us in every possible way.

I have thought that the reason why our dog was poisoned was for the purpose of having him out of the way so that they could place some of this bogus (evidence) somewhere on my premises.

P.S. Don't write much love, for the sheriff reads all letters.

May 6

The man who we are charged with conspiring with is but just alive here in jail and if he has told things to some of the R.R. folks, which they say he has, incriminating us from Jackson County, I do not wonder that he dies the death which he seems about to die, loathsome and disgusting in the extreme; however he may be innocent and the charges as corrupt and unjust against him as they are against us.

May 15

I have never placed a straw in the way of the Co. Only I have had the independence to tell them to their faces that they done wrong when they took the poor man's last cow without remuneration.

June 29

You no doubt get the testimony as it is given in court; did you ever conscience of anything so wicked? How foolish can anyone in Jackson County believe any of this, or that I (said) anything about burning depots?

We have got good lawyers and intend to do the best we can but to be far away from home locked up in a gloomy prison, what chance can we have for a fair trial?

Aug. 12

I want to see you again and be again at my peaceful home with my quiet little family. I remain so long as God gives me breath your devoted husband.

On the day he wrote these last lines, Fitch was struck with dysentery. He died 12 days later. In September, 12 men were convicted and sentenced to terms ranging from five to 10 years at hard labor. By 1855, one had died and the others had been pardoned. Seward was the top choice of Michigan Republicans for the party's 1860 presidential nomination, but lost to fellow Republican Abraham Lincoln. From the Abel F. Fitch papers in the Michigan Historical Collections at the University of Michigan's Bentley Historical Library.

1854 *'The great wrong must be righted'*

Slavery question boils over and the GOP is born

In 1854, the Kansas-Nebraska Act nullified the Missouri Compromise and opened new territories to slavery. The move brought a simmering national feud over slavery to a boil. Anti-slavery interests began looking for a unified political voice and some adherents placed an appeal, excerpted here, in Michigan newspapers.

A great wrong has been perpetrated. The slave power of the country has triumphed. Liberty is trampled underfoot. The Missouri Compromise, a solemn compact entered into by our fathers, has been violated, and a vast territory, dedicated to freedom, has been opened to slavery.

Northern Senators and Representatives have yielded to the seductions of executive patronage and, Judas-like, betrayed the cause of liberty; while the South, inspired by dominant and grasping ambition, has, without distinction of party and with a unanimity almost entire, deliberately trampled underfoot a solemn compact.

Such an outrage upon liberty, such a violation of plighted faith, cannot be submitted to. The great wrong must be righted, or there is no longer a North in the councils of the nation.

The extension of slavery under the folds of the American flag is a stigma upon liberty. The indefinite increase of slave representation in Congress is destructive to that equality between free men which is essential to the permanency of the Union.

The safety of the Union — the rights of the North — the interests of free labor — the destiny of a vast territory and its untold millions for all coming time — and, finally, the high aspirations of humanity for universal freedom, all are involved in the issue forced upon the country by the slave power and its plastic Northern tools.

In view, therefore, of the recent action of

Free Press files

Kinsley S. Bingham, Michigan's first Republican governor, was nominated at the convention.

59

Michigan Historical Collections, University of Michigan

This line cut shows the July 6, 1854 convention at Jackson.

Congress upon this subject, and the evident designs of the slave power to attempt still further aggressions upon freedom, we invite all our fellow citizens, without reference to former political associations, who think that the time has arrived for a union at the North to protect liberty from being overthrown and downtrodden, to assemble in

MASS CONVENTION
on
Thursday, the 6th of July next,
at 1 o'clock p.m.

AT JACKSON

there to take such measures as shall be thought best to concentrate the popular sentiment of this state against the aggression of slave power.

About 1,500 people attended that meeting, which became the first convention of the Republican Party and, in a sense, the founding of the party. Kinsley Bingham was nominated for governor at the convention, won the election and became Michigan's first Republican governor the next year. From William Stocking, "Under the Oaks," the Detroit Tribune, 1904: pages 39 and 40.

1862 'Cheers for the stars and stripes'

The North strikes a blow with handfuls of stones

One of only a few hundred Michigan sailors in the Civil War, Fowler Preston of St. Joseph was in the Brooklyn Navy Yard, assigned to the USS North Carolina. In a letter to his mother, Ann Jenette, he talks about his part in the war.

May 13, 1862

I sent you a paper last week that had all the news about Havana. There was 15 rebel boats in there when we was there flying the Stars and Bars.

We had a little affair last trip. While laying there, several boats pulled round our ship with the secession flag flying and shouting to us to haul down our old rag. We, having too much respect for the glorious Stars and Stripes, gathered a lot of small shot and stones and heaved them into their boats and hitting some of them, laid them up, for which our captain and our crew were ordered before the captain of the port to answer a charge of assault, which we did by dressing ourselves in white frocks and blue trousers and marched with our captain at our head, and after visiting the American consul, the captain sent us back with the purser to refresh ourselves and we all returned back, giving three loud cheers for the Stars and Stripes.

You wanted to know if I drank my ration of whisky. I didn't and I don't think you ever heard of my drinking anything strong and hope you never will as long as I live. You wanted to know if they pay our fare back home. I assure you they don't. If you have any money coming to you when you are paid off, well and good. If not, you must get along the best you can.

There is a great many one year's men getting their charge now. All the Cumberland crew was paid off last week. The Congress crew is aboard yet. They lost

Courtesy Arthur and Harriet Preston

Fowler Preston was one of only a few hundred Michigan men who became sailors in the Civil War.

everything they had and never got a cent for them.

How did Charles Sweet like the James Adger? She is a nice ship. That was the one I expected to go in. I shipped for her and another, but when they get you on the old North Carolina, they will do just what they please with you. I have had bad luck all the way through since I left home. I lost my bag of clothes and prize money. They will never pay me for the clothing that I lost.

You ask me if any hand is ever killed. It's not that scary. We have nothing to do, only stand lookout when we are outside. I have plenty of time to read. I got two pictures taken and will send them both home. How does Loren get along? I will write to Wallace (his older brother) next time. We sail again tomorrow. I suppose Wallace will own a vessel of his own before long. Well, it is about time, for he is quite able to. I think it is getting quite late in the afternoon, so I must come to an end. Give my best respects to all the boys.

Fowler Preston died in Chicago in 1896. The letters were submitted by Arthur and Harriet Preston of St. Joseph. Ann Jenette, who died in 1892, was Arthur Preston's great-grandmother.

1863 *'Expecting orders to march'*

Soldier describes sounds of the Civil War: Music among the guns and wagons

Finding some free time during the Civil War in March 1863, 2d Lt. Lucius "Lute" Shattuck, 26, wrote home to Plymouth from Camp Isabella, Va. His letter described leisure activities with Company C of the 24th Michigan Infantry Volunteers.

This has been a quiet Sabbath for camp. It used to seem to me that Sunday never came to the Army, or if it did it brought with it extra duties. Since we have been in winter quarters, however, it seems to have been the aim throughout the regiment to respect the day in a civilized manner. Sunday has still, however, a routine of duties, which it is the custom of the service to perform. For instance, regulations require an inspection of the troop, clothing, arms, ammunition and equipment and reports thereof filed in the adjutant's office.

The inspection and preparations for it consume the best part of the forenoon. The men usually have the remainder of the day to themselves, which, since there is not preaching, they employ in writing, reading and visiting. Sometimes we find them playing ball, perhaps cards, for want of something more interesting to them — I can, however, say of myself that I never had occasion to resort to games of any sort to pass away the time of Sundays. I am frequently obliged to draw and issue provisions such as fresh beef or fresh bread. Today I got a load of soft bread and issued it. Otherwise, I've spent the day in reading, chatting with the boys, writing this. Our shanty, being the fountain of supplies, is, like country stores, a favorite resort throughout the community.

After supper the regiment was called out to greet Gov. Oliver P. Morton of Indiana. He made a short patriotic speech in which he said he believed this rebellion would be crushed ere the close of June — I hope he

Free Press files

The flag of the 24th Michigan Infantry Volunteers after the battle at Gettysburg will prove a true prophet.

I often think of the Plymouth Brass Band and wonder if they still sustain themselves and how they progress.

We have a good band with our regiment which is a source of much pleasure. They enliven many an evening with their music. We also have a splendid brigade band — the third brigade whose headquarters are only about a hundred rods from here have also an excellent band of 15 pieces. Between the three we have music at almost every hour of the day.

We are constantly expecting orders to march. In fact, we have been prepared for two weeks past. The roads are not passable yet for heavy trains. Yesterday when I went over for the soft bread, I met a battery stuck in the mud on their way out for drill and inspection. A battery of only six-pounders too. We have no idea in what direction we shall go when we do move, though there are many conjectures. At any rate, we are willing to go wherever we may be needed and I for one would rather like to get out of Virginia.

Shattuck's company left Virginia and marched for Gettysburg, Pa. Early on July 1, the first day of the Battle of Gettysburg, Shattuck was wounded. His captain told him to have the wound dressed, but Shattuck stayed on the field. His diary, a hole shot through it, was later found on Seminary Ridge. His body is believed to have been buried in a mass grave. An estimated 48,000 were killed, wounded or reported missing during the battle, the turning point of the Civil War. From a letter submitted by the Plymouth Historical Museum.

State Archives, Michigan Dept. of State

This tent at the 1912 Michigan State Fair urged voting rights for women.

<u>1871</u> *'First drops of a coming shower'*

One woman votes and a city gasps in utter astonishment

Michigan newspapers in the spring of 1871 thoroughly reported the story of Nanette Gardner, a wealthy Detroit widow who had taken the revolutionary — and illegal — step of voting. But there was some debate as to whether Gardner or Mary Wilson of Battle Creek was the first woman to cast a ballot in Michigan. One judge even dug up the case of a Detroit widow who had voted in 1805. Gardner responded to the

uproar in a letter to the editor of the Detroit Post.

It is difficult for me to appreciate that so simple an event as a woman expressing a choice among a few candidates for office should have caused such a commotion and made me "suddenly famous." Tens of thousands of vicious, ignorant and worthless *men* do the same thing yearly without a word of comment. To an outsider, the inference would be quite plausible that women are something besides human beings — perhaps one of Darwin's apes suddenly emerging into and claiming the rights of humanity. Because two of us have succeeded in getting ourselves recognized as really "persons" upon the Constitution of our land, the telegraph is startled into action, millions stand aghast and an astute judge of our city has been digging up his charred and musty volumes to ascertain whether such a precedent had ever before been known.

The general expectation that women will soon universally vote, and their right to the ballot being only questioned by the same logic that slaves were denied their freedom, most rationally explains this phenomenon, and the few who begin to vote are regarded as the first drops of a coming shower.

While Miss Wilson may have voted earlier than myself, as you say by an hour, it is probably true that my name was the first registered. I should attach no importance to this and merely state it as a historical fact, if it should ever be noticed in history.

Few will dispute that our elections are carried by artful politicians either in the caucus or at the polls, more by cheap, debasing influences than by the wise and virtuous decisions of intelligent and honest citizens seeking to promote the public good. Officeholders, too, generally cling to and bribe the low and vulgar men who too often hold a majority of the ballots, and who, elected, use directly and indirectly the emoluments of the people to their own purposes. It is my firm belief that the women's vote will inaugurate a new era on the side of morality, economy, justice and competency. It will be "honor and glory" enough to have been instrumental in inaugurating it. When woman's power becomes effective, the keystone of that arch that now sustains the wily politician's structure will be knocked from its resting place, and the whole will tumble into a pile of splendid fragments.

It was nearly half a century before the 19th Amendment was approved, giving women the right to vote. Michigan became the first state to ratify the amendment, on June 10, 1919. From the June 3, 1871, issue of the Detroit Post.

1888 *'He continued to suffer'*

Civil War veteran's widow wins $8 a month in benefits

Simon Wertheimer, a cigar manufacturer on Woodbridge Street in Detroit, died on Dec. 25, 1888, and his widow, Bertha, filed for a pension as the widow of a Civil War veteran. Her husband had enlisted in Company A, 1st Infantry, on April 18, 1861, in Detroit. Although he served just a little more than three months, he fought in the worst part of the war, and friends said it ruined his health. To win the pension, Mrs. Wertheimer had to ask neighbors for comments about her late husband's health and her welfare.

Albert Polhemus: I am 56 years of age and I was well acquainted with the late soldier Simon S. Wertheimer. I saw him when he first came home from the service. At that time he was in very poor health, suffering with pain in the chest and weakness of lungs. I often heard him complain of how much he suffered with his lungs. He was never able to do any hard work and he was often laid up and unable to do anything at all. I saw him on an average of twice a week from the time he came home from the service to the time of his death in December 1888, and I know that he continued to suffer with lung disease the entire time.

O.E. Botsford: I became acquainted with the above-mentioned soldier in 1875. At the time of my first acquaintance, and thereafter until he died, he was troubled with disease of lungs and a bad cough. He would frequently be seized with coughing spells, at which time he would nearly strangle. I often advised him to apply for pension on account of said disability, as he said it began in the Army, but he neglected to do so. He often took medicines for his cough and doctored with several physicians on account of same.

Samuel Van Baalen: (I) have been

Courtesy Lois Wertheimer Lipnik

Simon S. Wertheimer

Courtesy Lois Wertheimer Lipnik

Simon S. Wertheimer stands on the left in the doorway to his Detroit cigar factory. A sign advertises the "best 5¢ cigar in America."

acquainted with claimant for the past 10 years. She has not married since the date of the death of her husband, the late Simon S. Wertheimer. Further, claimant has no property and has no instrument of any kind which yields her an income, and in consequence she is dependent on her daily labor for support; also on the assistance of others not legally bound for her support.

The letters apparently did the job. Bertha Wertheimer won a widow's pension, and in July 1890, the government began paying her $8 a month. By the time of her death on Feb. 10, 1926, the pension had been increased to $30 a month. From letters submitted by Lois Wertheimer Lipnik, great-granddaughter of Simon and Bertha Wertheimer.

Here to stay

"To go back to Germany and stay there I will not do. I know beforehand that I would not like it there and I would not fit in anymore."
— Friedrich Ruffertshoefer

1857 'The miseries of school teaching'

New students every day; a new home every night

In 1857, Michigan schoolhouses were one-room affairs and teachers, primarily young women, were paid $3 or $4 a week in winter and about $2 a week during the two-month summer sessions. Teachers boarded at pupils' homes, a nomadic existence that Elizabeth Wilcox, 22, a homesick teacher in Macomb County, wrote about in a pocket-sized notebook at the end of each day.

July 5

Mr. Cone came for me. I was soon ready and in a short time arrived at my new home, when I was possessed with a feeling of loneliness which I could not overcome. And tomorrow morning I am to enter upon my duties for the coming summer. 'Tis a dread.

July 6

A little more reconciled to my lot. Today I met eight of the scholars that are to be trusted in my care for a few weeks. Eight strange faces and as many different dispositions to become acquainted with.

July 10

At Mr. Hill's again tonight. Oh dear me, the miseries of school teaching. Here am I, afflicted most to death with the toothache. And what is still worse, I have been obliged to play sociable for the last two hours. But to every day there follows a bedtime and how glad I am it has come so early tonight. Now I am left to myself. No one to speak to me and if there was, I should be uncivil enough not to answer.

July 11

Back again at Mr. Cone's. It is almost as good a home as my own. I could ask for no better, at least no person can find better when away from their own home and friends.

July 13

Today had five new scholars. Tonight am

Courtesy Bev Leese
Elizabeth Wilcox taught in Macomb County until 1862, when she moved to a farm near Port Huron.

to Mr. Gibson's. I made my appearance unexpected to them as the little boy forgot to tell them I was coming.

July 14

Tonight went to Mr. Brant's from school. Never before has my courage so failed me as it did the moment I entered his house. Mrs. B. came running up as though she was going to take off my bonnet and shawl for me and at last pointed me to a seat. I soon found there was to be no formalities as each one was to help themselves. (After dinner) a brother of Mr. B's came. Just returned from Kansas. Also two gent. from Detroit and one from the old country. All gentlemanly appearing Dutchmen. All was gibberish and jabbering, and this with the tobacco smoke which I had to endure, for all were smoking. Was a little more than I could stand, so I excused myself to Mrs. B. and made my way back to Mr. Cone and here I shall spend the remainder of the night unless there is an army of Dutchmen coming or something else of importance to prevent.

Elizabeth Wilcox evidently overcame her homesickness. She taught in Macomb County until 1862, when she married Charles King and moved to a farm near Port Huron. She died in 1925 at age 91. Her diary and photograph were submitted by her great-granddaughter, Bev Leese of Birmingham.

Courtesy Emery and
Katheryn Seestedt
Eliza Moore earned $47.50 plus
room and board for teaching
three months in Smithville.

<u>**1866**</u> *'Scholars of all ages and sizes'*

With 89 students in class, the room gets crowded

*In 1866, Reconstruction was under way
in the South, croquet was a popular game in
the East and, in Detroit, James Vernor
came out with a new brand of ginger ale.
Eliza Moore was living on her family's
homestead farm between Belleville and
Pullen's Corners, now Romulus, when word
came that nearby Smithville needed a
teacher.*

Jan. 2

Father and Jasper (her brother)
butchered three hogs and started with two of
them for Detroit about 9 o'clock this
evening. I don't envy our folks their ride to
Detroit tonight.

Jan. 3

Our folks came home about dark, cold,

71

tired, hungry and sleepy, which is apt to be the case in riding so far. They sold their pork for $11 per hundredweight. Oats 37 cents per bushel; butter 31 cents per lb., eggs 35 cents per doz. Mother and I knitting in the evening. Our folks gone to bed.

Jan. 6

J.L. from Smithville came here in search of teacher for Smithville school, their teacher having left.

Jan. 18

About 11 o'clock Mr. B. from Smithville came to see me about teaching school there. I agreed to teach for $5 per week and board to commence next Monday.

Jan. 21

Very cold this morning, almost too cold to venture out, but teachers must go (in) all kinds of weather. Father started about noon and had rather a cold ride. The roads are (so) icy that it is very hard traveling for a horse.

Jan. 22

School commenced this morning. I have 25 scholars of all ages and sizes. They are strictly speaking rather a rough set, but I hope they will improve. There is plenty of room for improvement. One of the inspectors called at school this morning. He asked me some questions this evening and is to give me a certificate.

Jan. 29

Instead of washing day as usual, it is school day. I have several large boys who all seem to try to study, for which I am very glad. I was intending to go to Mr. L tonight but it is so sloppy that I went to Mr. B, which is not so far from the schoolhouse. I have now 38 — rather a larger school than expected.

Jan. 31

Some colder this morning and not as good a fire at the schoolhouse as Freddie generally has.

Feb. 5

Now have all the scholars that the schoolhouse can conveniently hold and now I have to crowd them together as I have 89 names.

Feb. 9

Another sleigh ride to school this morning. I am lucky. School has passed off as usual except the smoke the stovepipe has given out and we had more smoke than I agreed for, but it was not as bad as might be.

Feb. 20

A teacher living around has a good opportunity of observing the government of children. How many different ways there is of doing the same thing and no two persons govern alike. I can tell by being a short time in a house whether obedience from children is through love or fear, and there are some who have no government at all. I like to see people at home to judge of their good qualities or bad ones. Some have two faces, one for home and one for abroad. The face at home is usually clouded by a frown and every word is harsh. But while they are away, smiles are on their faces always, and all say what a pleasant person that is, but little do they know the real character.

In 1868, Eliza Moore married Zurial Monroe, a Civil War veteran who served in the 5th Michigan Cavalry under Gen. George Custer. These excerpts were submitted by Emery M. Seestedt of Marine City, a grandson, and his wife, Katheryn.

Courtesy Reinhold and Marie Block

This log house, shown near Frankenmuth in 1863, was typical of homes of that time.

1867 *'I would not fit in anymore'*

German farmer has nothing to fear from robbers, Indians or bears

A wave of immigration in the 1860s nearly tripled Michigan's population from 450,000 to 1.2 million. About 50,000 of those people came from overseas. One was Friedrich Ruffertshoefer, who sailed in 1867 from Langenfeld, Germany, and began carving a farm out of the wilderness near Frankenmuth. He wrote to his parents in Germany about his new country.

(The road) leads to Saginaw, 14 miles away. Since there are no stones available for road building, but enough wood, the roads are covered with boards and planks. That this makes for a good ride, you can very well imagine. I live about one mile north of this road.

Two portions of 80 acres each are owned by Bierlein and myself. The land is pure and genuine virgin forest. There is not even a small place the size of a room without trees. That does not bother me in the least. I can handle it, if God is kind enough to grant me life, strength and good health. My ax is sharp enough and wherever the wood is dry enough, fire will show its might. I also hope my dear Barbara will help me conquer the woods with her strong arms. Sure, it will mean a great deal of work to cut down those trees, some of which have been growing God only knows since when. I would hate to do the work with a German ax.

Things would have been much easier for me had I married the Schwartz girl instead of the Weiss girl. The Schwartz girl owns a nice 100-acre farm. But it never occurred to me to take for my wife a redheaded, frivolous 16-year-old girl that still smells of the midwife.

I do not live in a wilderness, dear parents; you do not need to worry about that. There also is no danger from robbers, simply because I do not own anything of value and that kind of people is not to be found in these parts anyway. The Indians also are absolutely no danger to me, since they lead a rather wretched life. They are as tame as a house cat and are glad if left alone. Also there are no wild animals around. I really would like to meet up with a bear. I would shoot the beast and get a good sum of money for it.

People do not live together in a village as they do in Germany. Everybody lives on his own land. That is very convenient and practical. The distance to the work in the field is much shorter this way. All the land is fenced in, so the cattle can roam freely and cannot get off your land. That makes it much easier for women's work — no carting of grass to the animals, the cattle can graze all day and night.

To go back to Germany and stay there I will not do. I know beforehand that I would not like it there and I would not fit in anymore. I got so used to life here, the way things are done in this country, the manners and the customs here, that I would have a difficult time in Germany to change things back to the old ways.

From a letter in a collection of copies donated to the Frankenmuth Historical Association in 1983 by Johannes Georg Freyman of West Germany.

1878 *'A nice bedroom over the kitchen'*

Maid is happy to earn $3 a week washing, cooking and serving

Juliana Heath, 33, a native of England, came to Detroit in November 1878, after living three years in Cashmere, Ontario. In these letters to her sister, Mary Ann, she described life as a maid for the family of U.S. Circuit Judge Halmor Emmons in their house on Henry Street.

Nov. 7, 1878

I like these people very well but I have got lots of work to do, but it is not every poor little girl in Detroit that gets $3 a week.

Detroit is a large city, very clean, with wide streets and stone sidewalks. I must introduce you to Susie, the girl that is living here. She has not been living here long and she thinks it is dreadful lonesome so far from the middle of the city. The streetcars cross the street a little way from the house.

The front part of the house is heated with hot air and we have got a nice bedroom over the kitchen with a drum in the stove pipe.

Jan. 8, 1879

Miss Emmons is hard on the fellows that work for her. There is an old Frenchman that came to fix things around the house and was always trying to kiss Susie, so she made him believe one day that she had told Miss Emmons of him and that she was going to lecture him, and Napolean said we be too frightened of that little girl, we had ought to go for her and give her a licking. Susie has left us and gone to live at Gov. Balldons. (Heath probably was referring to Henry Baldwin, who was governor from 1869 to 1872.) It is one of the largest houses in Detroit. They keep two house maids and two colored gents livery and two colored ladies for cooks. Mrs. Emmons thought that she was going away at the beginning of this month and Susie was engaged to go and they would not wait any longer of her. There is a girl coming tomorrow to do the cooking and I

Burton Historical Collection, Detroit Public Library

The Emmons house where Juliana Heath lived and worked is now gone.

am going to do the upstairs work for the same pay.

Mrs. E. says that she thinks that they will like me around them. They wanted me to do the upstairs work when I first came (but) thought that such a little mite as me could not do the washing. But I have done it and the ironing and the cooking and waiting at table and I have had to try the other work in the morning. I often think of what I once read about two angels, if one came to this world to sweep a street and another to rule the city they would both try to do their work well.

Juliana Heath married Alexander McFarlane in 1881 and lived near Chatham, Ontario, until her death in 1918. From letters submitted by her brother's great-grandson, Guy St. Denis of London, Ontario.

75

1881 'Smoke rolled over the village'

Racing, leaping walls of flame destroy whole families

The summer of 1881 was unusually dry in Michigan's parched Thumb and tangled accumulations of dried stumps and slashings, the legacy of the logging era, made people fear of a conflagration. On Sept. 5, it struck. Readers opening to Page 2 of the Sept. 6 Port Huron Daily Times found the first reports from the fire.

SCOURGED BY FIRE

A large portion of Huron and Sanilac Counties burned over Monday afternoon — hundreds of families lose everything and scores of lives lost — a few scattering details and more horrors to be heard from.

Some time must elapse before the full details can be collected, but enough is already known to warrant the assertion that a more terrible disaster never visited any community in a time of peace.

Mr. Jacob Springer arrived down on the steamer M.D. Ward this morning. He says that at 11 o'clock Monday dense volumes of smoke rolled over the village, and at noon it was as dark as night, lamps were lighted, and men went about the streets with lanterns.

Mr. J.W. Benedict, who came down on the Ward this morning, brings the report that 40 persons were burned to death in Paris Township, Huron County, and 13 lives were lost southwest of Sand Beach.

Mr. Springer says he thought on Monday that he should never see Port Huron again. He left Minden Tuesday morning with a horse and buggy, in company with another man, and they had a hard time getting through to Forestville. On the way they saw horses, cattle, sheep and other animals roasted by the roadside.

Two and a half miles above Deckerville the rails have been twisted so badly by the heat that the train could not run.

The postmaster at Elmer sent back the

American Red Cross

The flames killed whole families and reportedly overtook running horses.

horse of the mail carrier between Marlette and that place, with a card attached to his sack, saying that the mail carrier had been burned to death on the way.

A man went into a burning house and took two children from a bed, carried them two or three miles, and through exhaustion had to leave them. Someone carried them two miles further through the smoke and flame, wearied out, and left them by the roadside, where they perished.

The fire burned 2,000 square miles, killed 280 people and left 15,000 homeless. It also signaled the end of the lumber era in the Thumb and the start of the agricultural age. Copies of the Port Huron Daily Times and recollections of the fire were gathered for "Fiery Trial," a book by James H. Lincoln and James L. Donahue, published by the Historical Society of Michigan in 1984.

76

American Red Cross

Many families fled with what they could carry, trying to outrun the fire or find safety in rivers or Lake Huron.

Courtesy Leonora Carpenter

Leonora Crowell came to Iron Mountain as a newlywed and stayed the rest of her life.

1882 *'In two seconds . . . man and wife'*

$2 and a promise are plenty in a booming iron town

Newlyweds Leonora Crowell, 23, and Dr. J. Addison Crowell, 28, moved in 1882 to booming Iron Mountain, where Dr. Crowell joined another doctor's practice. There were no houses to rent or buy then, not even for the new doctor in town, so the Crowells lived in a single room at the Jenkins Hotel. In a letter to her younger sister Dora at home in New Jersey, Mrs. Crowell wrote about a wedding in Michigan's iron country, just 40 days after her own.

Last evening being Saturday, the Drs. took their clean underclothes, done up in paper, up with them to the office, where they have a nice bathroom with hot and cold water for the hospital patients. After office hours they, the Drs., each take a good bath, put on their clean clothes and then come home. We, the Mrs. Drs., get each a pitcher of hot water from the girls in the kitchen and wash in the same old way as we have to at home.

Well, I had taken my wash and had put on my clean clothes, and nightdress too: had just taken down my hair to cut off a little more of the bang when Mrs. P. knocked at my door. She told me there was a couple in the parlor waiting for the "justice" to arrive for they were to be married. Well, says I, can we go and see it done? I never dressed so quickly in my life. Hair and all had to be fixed. So we were present at the marriage, and what a form to be called so!

A dingy uncombed justice of the peace sat at the center table. His name I believe was Rackerty, and he looked just like his name. The couple stood up in front of the table, and Mr. Jenkins and one of the dining-room girls stood with them. The bride was a bold-looking girl of 29 — very large for her age. The groom more modest and 24 years old. He was so worked up that the perspiration stood out in large drops all over his forehead. They had to hold up their right hands and swear to answer the questions put to them truthfully; such as, were they ever married before? Were they any relation to each other? What was their names, occupation, age, etc., then they were told to put down their hands and join hands and in two seconds they were man and wife. All the old fellow said, or about all, was, "Now according to the laws of Michigan and before these witnesses you are man and wife."

The fellow sat down nervously, put his hand in his pocket, then got up and asked, "How much?" "Two dollars," said old Rackerty. Out came two silver dollars. Then his hand went back again into the pocket and fished out 50 cents. That he handed over to the old fellow too, and told him it was for to get a smoke with.

(Later) the young fellows boarding here all got together — I mean all but the decent ones, and they are very few up in this rough country — downstairs and cheered the bride, for they had heard of her being upstairs.

The Crowells built a home in Iron Mountain and had four daughters and a son. They named one daughter Leonora, and she also named a daughter Leonora. That woman, Nora Carpenter, is in her 70s and lives in the house that her grandparents built. She allowed the Mid-Peninsula Library Federation, at Iron Mountain, to publish her grandmother's letters as a book in 1976.

1891 *'The money . . . is always sure'*

The hours are long and hot stoking on the Soo Line

George Ward and Ann Jane Buck married in Michigan's Upper Peninsula in 1891, the year Thomas Edison received patents on the motion picture camera and the radio and the year James Naismith invented basketball. In letters to his fiancee, Ward described life as a fireman on the "Soo Line," the Minneapolis, St. Paul & Sault Ste. Marie Railroad.

May 22, 1891

We left Gladstone yesterday at noon and reached (Gilchrist) at 6 p.m. It is about 75 miles from the Soo and is right in the woods. There is only one house besides the railroad buildings, which are a coal shed, water tank, pump house and depot.

My work is to watch the engine nights, clean her and fire her up in the morning and have steam up at 6 a.m. for a start. She is hauling logs.

Aug. 8, 1891

We moved to (Cooks Mills) from Gilchrist four or five days ago and our next move will be to Mattison siding. I don't know whether I will get back to the shop then or not. I prefer to stay out. I get better pay and have more chance to learn how to fire.

This is a small place: a sawmill, store and post office, two saloons and two boarding houses. The one where I board is kept by an old colored gentleman and his wife. There is a daughter-in-law and two little black kids visiting here now. Their name is Bass and they are pretty black and are *nice* people, very intelligent seemingly and give pretty fair board.

We have run a good many miles and loaded a good many hundred ties since we left Gladstone and have a lot more of it.

The engineer and fireman of this engine are both married men, and their wives came out to see them this week and remained overnight. They think I am the queerest stick they ever saw. Don't take any beer, cigars, tabac in any form, don't get stuck on the shape of any of the ladies and attend to my own business generally. The fireman was saying he would do so-and-so and I wouldn't. Well, I said, you see, Jack, that's just the difference between you and a man. The engineer laughed for half an hour at the take-off, as he called it, and Jack subsided.

After the wedding, Ann Jane described George's job in a letter to her brother, Thomas Buck.

Dec. 31, 1891

(George) was working on the yard engine then at nights, but Monday night he was sent to Pennington, awakened at 12:20 by the dispatcher and had to leave depot at 12:40. He got back home Wednesday morning at 7:30 and went direct to bed and two hours later, along came that *terrible* dispatcher again. And the poor fellow, after being up all night and half of the night before, had to get up and go at 10:45. I tell you, Tom, there isn't any fun in being a railroad man, or in being his wife, either.

Well, yes, there is at the end of the month — payday. The money comes in cash and is always sure. When he worked at night he got $1.76 per night; he gets when on the road $2.20 per 100 miles.

George became an engineer on the Soo Line and was killed Aug. 7, 1912, when his train ran into an open switch. He was 47. Ann Jane died four years later at 51. Her letter was submitted by Thomas Buck's granddaughter, Lou MacGready of Swartz Creek. Her search for photographs led to Gladstone and George and Ann Jane's great-granddaughter, Sharon Ivory, who submitted the first two letters.

Courtesy Sharon Ivory

George Ward is on the right in this 1910 photograph of a Soo Line engine.

Courtesy Sharon Ivory
George Ward and Anne Jane Buck

1893 *'They swarmed on all our coasts'*

Native American can only weep over Columbus' discovery

A proud America held its Columbian Exhibition in Chicago in 1893 and invited Simon Pokagon of Hartford, Mich., as guest of honor for "Chicago Week." Pokagon's father, Potawatomi Chief Leopold Pokagon, had signed the 1833 Chicago Treaty that deeded over the land on which the fairgrounds stood. It was cruel irony to be a "guest" on that land, but Pokagon attended and distributed a tiny booklet printed on birch bark. He called it "The Red Man's Rebuke."

"Shall not one line lament our race,
For you struck out from wild creation's face?
Freedom — the selfsame freedom you adore,
Bade us defend our violated shore."

In behalf of my people, the American Indians, I hereby declare to you, the pale-faced race that has usurped our lands and homes, that we have no spirit to celebrate with you the great Columbian Fair now being held in this Chicago city, the wonder of the world.

No; sooner would we hold high joy-day over the graves of our departed fathers, than to celebrate our own funeral, the discovery of America. And while you who are strangers, and you who live here, bring the offerings of the handiwork of your own lands, and your hearts in admiration rejoice over the beauty and grandeur of this young republic, and you say, "Behold the wonders brought by our children in this foreign land," do not forget that this success has been at the sacrifice of *our* homes and a once-happy race.

Where these great Columbian show buildings stretch skyward, and where stands the "Queen City of the West," *once* stood the red man's wigwam; here met their old men, young men and maidens; here blazed their council fires. But now the eagle's eye can find no trace of them. Here was the center of their widespread hunting grounds; stretching far eastward, and to the great salt Gulf southward, and to the lofty Rocky Mountain chain westward, and all about and beyond the Great Lakes northward, roamed vast herds of buffalo that no man could number, while moose, deer and elk were found from ocean to ocean; pigeons, ducks and geese in near bow-shot moved in great clouds through the air, while fish swarmed our streams, lakes and seas close to shore. All were provided by the Great Spirit for our use; we destroyed none except for food and dress; had plenty and were contented and happy.

But alas! The palefaces came by chance to our shores, many times very needy and hungry. We nursed and fed them — fed the ravens that were soon to pluck out our eyes and the eyes of our children; for no sooner had the news reached the Old World that a new continent had been found, peopled with another race of men, than, locust-like, they swarmed on all our coasts.

The cyclone of civilization spread westward; the forests of untold centuries were swept away; streams dried up; lakes fell back from their ancient bounds; and all our fathers once loved to gaze upon was destroyed, defaced, or marred, except the sun, moon and starry skies above, which the Great Spirit in his wisdom hung beyond their reach.

You say of us that we are treacherous, vindictive and cruel; in answer to the charge we declare to all the world that before the white man came among us, we were kind, outspoken and forgiving. Our real character has been misunderstood because we have resented the breaking of treaties made with

Burton Historical Collection, Detroit
Public Library

Simon Pokagon, who told white
celebrants at Chicago how
America had been taken from
his people.

the United States, as we honestly
understood them.

We never shall be happy here anymore;
we gaze into the faces of our little ones, for
smiles of infancy to please, and into the faces
of our young men and maidens, for joys of
youth to cheer advancing age, but alas!
Instead of smiles of joy we find but looks of
sadness there. Then we fully realize in the
anguish of our souls that their young and
tender hearts, in keenest sympathy with
ours, have drank in the sorrows we have felt,
and their sad faces reflect it back to us again.

*From Simon Pokagon's "The Red Man's
Rebuke," published by C.H. Engle,
Hartford, Mich., in 1893.*

83

1893 'Crowds of men ... waiting'

In the midst of a depression, a wedding lifts hearts

In February 1893, the Philadelphia & Reading Railroad went bankrupt, starting a panic and stock market collapse that, by year's end, ruined 16,000 U.S. businesses and 500 banks and threw the country into a depression. In Detroit, Mayor Hazen Pingree earned the name "Potato Pingree" for letting the unemployed farm vacant land and selling his riding horse at auction to pay for seeds. A woman in Detroit described the bleakness of the times and the merriment of a wedding in this letter, written Nov. 21, 1893.

I was going to write Sunday, but when I went to church, sat behind a woman who had just brought out her sealskin cloak from its summer retirement of gasoline, chloroform, ether, etc. I thought there was gas escaping in the room. But only we in the seat behind that cloak smelled it and it felt as if I was having gas to have my teeth out. Well, it made me sick for the rest of the day so I could not go out in the evening.

It is a horrible day today. Snow and thaw and I think it is raining now. I had to go to town for some blue jean to hang up in a doorway and so managed to get skirts and ankles wet, so am snuffing camphor. For a change we all keep well and I suppose one ought to "count their mercies" if they can see them.

I tell you, if you could see the crowds of men standing in front of the city hall with their shovels and picks waiting for something to do, it might make you feel a little nervous, if you began to think what they might do when they grew desperate. One (railroad) car shop which employed 3,000 men has 200 at work. The Pullman, where there were between 1,000 and 2,000, only has the watchman and engineer, and so it goes. Frank took your advice and deposited the money instead of paying for

Free Press files

Mayor Hazen S. Pingree was known as "Potato Pingree" for encouraging farming on empty lots in Detroit.

the lot (a home site). And it is fortunate, for we will have to draw from it for next month's rent. But we are so much more fortunate than two-thirds the rest, for many had nothing to fall back on.

There were between 80 and 90 people (at the wedding) and, for all it was such a horrid day, everyone was jolly. They had an arch of evergreen in one corner with a pot of red and one of yellow chrysanthemums at the ends. They had boards about 30 inches long and 18 wide that four or five could take on their lap. Then Amy and Rena passed towels to spread on them, then they passed plate, napkins, forks and cups. They had coffee, tea, and chocolate, raised biscuits, pressed chicken, boiled ham, pickles, olives, egg salad, fruit cake, gold and silver chocolate cake and bride's cake, ice cream and squares of cake with pink frosting and a nut meat in the center of each. We rode in an open buggy from the station to the house and faced the wind. I don't really know if I'm warmed through yet, but a round oak stove and plenty of wood kept things humming.

The car shops referred to in the letter probably made railroad cars, as Detroit's first auto plant was about 2½ years away. "The Pullman" likely was the plant for George Pullman's railroad cars, which moved to Chicago about this time. This letter was submitted by Lori Heglin of Mt. Clemens, who collects old letters.

Bernard Historical Society and Museum

Hannah Collier Falk, right, in front of her house with a friend, about 1896.

1896 *'Awatching for the rockets'*

Liberty poles, pranks and dynamite greet McKinley's election

In a diary filled with notes on family, friends and home life in rural southwest Michigan, Hannah Collier Falk noted highlights on the local political scene. The 1896 election was one of the hardest-fought presidential contests in history, pitting Republican William McKinley against "free silver" candidate William Jennings Bryan.

Oct. 28

It rained this forenoon till about noon. We took Dixie and Jerry and we went over to Delton to a torchlight Republican rally. Mr. Victor M. Gore from Benton Harbor was a splendid speaker. The speech was in the schoolhouse. I saw lot of folks over there.

Oct. 29

I am to Frances (a daughter) this forenoon. I went across the field to Nettie's (another daughter), was there to dinner. I took care of Opal and Rankin (two of her grandchildren) and Nettie went down to my house and went with Iva Donivon to Dr. Capps and she had eight teeth drawn and took gas. Then Nettie had one of hers filled over. Lottie cooked apples and boiled down cider. Opal and I, we picked up hickory nuts, not many for they are (as scarce as) hen's teeth. Adelbert Blackman's store raided tonight, found the door open in the morning.

Some shoes and cigars and some other small things missing.

Oct. 31

Halloween night tonight. I am to Nettie's yet today. Dr. Hyde (Nettie's husband, George) has gone to Hastings to get his naturalization papers, so he can vote Nov. 3, 1896, for William McKinley of the United States of America.

Nov. 1

It was a beautiful day today. The boys tore around quite a little last night, their Halloween. They made a man and stuffed it and were going to hang it on the Democrat pole and call it Mr. Bryan, but Mr. Higgins would not let them do so. (Poles made of spliced wooden rails, some more than 150 feet high, were common at election time. They had banners bearing the names of candidates.)

Nov. 2

Lots of folks has gone tonight to Kalamazoo to hear Julius C. Burrows speak at the Academy of Music, a hard-money, goldbug Republican. I gave Birdie a nice plate handle today. I wrote a letter and put steels in my corset tonight and read in my papers.

Nov. 3

I patched two of my flannel shirts. Today is election day. Willie Merlau (her 22-year-old grandson) here and stayed all night, so he could know how the election goes. Dr. Hyde and Temple and Nelson is attending to the telephone from Augusta about the election and the men in the hall is counting the votes. They have had a big bonfire all night and singing and dancing and they are awatching for the rockets to go up from Kalamazoo. Willie comes down every half-hour and brings the news from the telephone in the store. I went to the store and got three yards of red flannel, 75 cents. Sarah, Iva and I went uptown tonight to see Bryan hung to the Democrat pole. They are a having a big jubilee downtown tonight. They exploded dynamite twice this morning.

Bernard Historical Society and Museum

Hannah Collier Falk in about 1896.

Nov. 4

McKinley has got a big majority for president.

Nov. 5

Carl Loveland in Hughes field exploded dynamite. They fired it off three times. It made my bedroom window rattle last night.

Hannah Collier Falk was 64 when she wrote about the election. Despite her interest, she was no more than a spectator. Women did not have the right to vote until the 19th Amendment was ratified in 1920. The diary was submitted by the Bernard Historical Society and Museum in Delton, Barry County.

Courtesy Elizabeth Greene Gibbs

Charles Edward Greene and Emma Waterloo Greene about the time of his 1887 graduation from the University of Michigan's medical school.

1906 *'The wife gave the anesthetic'*

'Mrs. Doctor' lends a hand, draws line at pulling teeth

Emma Waterloo Greene was married to Charles Greene, a doctor in St. Clair and Macomb Counties, and told what it was like to be the wife of a country doctor around the turn of the century. She gave this talk before the Richmond, Mich., Literary Club in 1906.

I never had it in my mind to marry a doctor, lawyer, merchant or chief — but just get a suitable man and make out of him for what he was most suited, for that is what I did. "Medicine" did not start in our family until after we had talked it over and decided that was best. I not only have had the experience of the doctor's wife, but also of the student's wife. I know about the drudgery and the anxieties of the medical student. I early knew the smell of chemicals in our sitting room and have many a time slept with a skeleton or some anatomical specimen stowed carefully under my bed, because there was no other place for it.

I could tell you of glad days and sad days

and lonely days, too. Glad days when the sick people were recovering and the baby forgot to be cross, and the sun shone on all the world. Sad days when there seemed to be no sunshine anywhere, for the good people we had learned to love were taken from us in spite of all that could be done. And lonely days and nights when my own babies were sick and I felt very desolate, indeed. For, of course, at such times someone miles away would be sure to need the doctor and he would have to go. So, you see, the other woman would have her husband and her doctor, while I had neither. Perhaps the next day a neighbor would tell me how fortunate I was to have a doctor in the family. She forgot the old saying about the shoemaker's children.

Sometimes the people seemed to think if the doctor were not at home, "Mrs. Doctor" would do just as well, if not better. In fact, they have told me more than once that my medicine helped them more than the doctor's had. And I don't doubt but it did. I made cough medicine and ointment, refilled old prescriptions and dealt out pills. But I did draw the line at extracting teeth. No doubt, though, after a little practice, I might have become an expert and hardened as — I don't say whom — who at first thought only of the pain he was giving, but after a little said his only thought was, "I wonder if I'll get paid?"

It isn't always easy to be properly sympathetic when a tiresome woman insists on you seeing and hearing all about the sore on Johnny's head and how Mary cut her finger and the baby fell downstairs, when you can smell your bread burning in the oven and know that your jam is boiling over, and you are not sure but in your haste to answer the doorbell you forgot to cover the cistern around which the children are playing.

Neither do you enjoy, just as you get into your best bib and tucker and start for church, thinking you will have a quiet hour away from it all, being called back to give an anesthetic to a dirty, ugly, imp of Satan, while the doctor probes in her ear for a long lost kernel of corn.

Like the minister's wife, I was expected to be ready at all times to give what I could of assistance or sympathy in the house of mourning, when the baby had convulsions, or Jimmie broke his arm, and various other times.

And then the unexpected things that happen! When nature is smiling and serene there comes a report of a sudden illness or accident, and immediately the office, if not the whole house, is transformed as if by magic into a hospital. Bandages are hastily prepared, dressing and instruments sterilized and antiseptic solutions prepared. Perhaps the doctor's wife gave the anesthetic and helped make the patient more comfortable, then quietly resumed her duties of housekeeping.

On one occasion of an emergency operation, the wife gave the anesthetic and her little boy of seven or eight handed the doctor the instruments as they were needed and used the sponges to keep the field of operation free from blood. The case should have gone to the hospital, had there been one available.

Charles Greene, who graduated from the University of Michigan in 1887 and Long Island College Hospital in 1890, was elected to the Michigan Senate in 1925. The boy mentioned in the last paragraph, Irving Waterloo Greene, grew up to become a doctor. His daughter, Elizabeth Greene Gibbs of Owosso, submitted this account.

Water,
wood and rock

"The average human imagination becomes temporarily diseased when stimulated by the chances of possessing hidden mineral wealth. Iron, being the least valuable of the metals, has less of this influence than the others, but it is not entirely free from it."
— T.B. Brooks

1846 'Persons arriving in every boat'

Copper fever drives thousands to the Upper Peninsula

In 1846 the first telegraph line was strung from New York to Washington, D.C., astronomers discovered the planet Neptune and a new game, called baseball, was introduced. In Michigan, copper fever was raging and George Cannon, a 19-year-old from Bruce, in Macomb County, caught it. He set off from Detroit in the spring as part of American Exploring Co., bound for the Copper Country.

May 10

Hundreds of persons (are) arriving (at Sault Ste. Marie) in every boat, destined for the mineral region. Some 30 or 40 tents were bivouacked at the head of the rapids, with the continual roll of wheels conveying baggage across the portage giving to the scene a busy appearance. The schooner Fur Trader was chartered by the company party to convey the parties to their destinations, and after many vexatious delays, the wind having proved fair, we were on board.

May 24

We arose this morning early, thoroughly drenched, and had experienced what our voyageurs called a good specimen of camping out. The sun rose pleasant and the morning is warm, which seemed to be appreciated by one kind of animal life in particular; for immense swarms of blackflies, thicker than the leaves in the forest, hovered around our divine faces and proceeded to demand blood, without the least ceremony as to where or how they obtained it. They were so thick that it was nearly impossible to eat a meal without eating, as the voyageurs called it, an extra supply of seasoning.

July 20

We were exploring the mountain, which on its south side is precipitous and broken.

From "History, Macomb County, Michigan Illustrated, 1882"

George Cannon became a teacher and surveyor.

Lying along its base are large quantities of broken rock that had fallen down from the high ledge above. Scrambling our way along these fallen masses, we came to the ledge, which is composed of trap rock, very compact and of a deep bluish color.

July 21

Today we ran out another location of the same size as the other, joining it on the east. The remainder of the party were exploring the vein, which has considerable of a dip to the north, and lying parallel with the range, which has a direction nearly east and west. The vein appears to be very rich and the men obtained from it several pieces of native copper, one of which weighed 110 pounds. Some of the men were so much delighted with the present prospects that they did not pretend to sleep and, accordingly, sat up near all night around the campfire, smoking their pipes and telling stories, which gave to the camp an unusual hilarity.

George Cannon returned to lower Michigan and became a teacher at Rochester, but went on several surveying trips in the 10 years after his first trip to the Copper Country. His diary was published by the family as "A Narrative of One Year in the Wilderness" in 1982 and was submitted by grandson Guy Cannon and his wife, Carrie.

U.S. Army Corps of Engineers, Detroit

A steamer leaving Lake Superior is in the lower of the two original locks, about 1875.

1853 *'Delays . . . have been very many'*

Distance, diarrhea, competition plague Soo Canal builders

Pressure to build locks so ships could negotiate the 22-foot drop from Lake Superior to Lake Huron grew with every pound of ore that had to be unloaded, carted around the St. Mary's River and reloaded for the trip down the lakes. The job was not an easy one, though. Much of the canal had to be cut through solid rock and the area was remote. Sen. Henry Clay, upon hearing of the project, said, "it is a work quite beyond the remotest settlement of the United States, if not in the moon."

Charles Harvey, in charge of construction at the Soo for the St. Mary's Falls Ship Canal Co., had been working on the canal for 16 weeks and had heard grumbling that he would miss the May 19, 1855, deadline. Harvey defended himself in this letter to attorney James Joy, an officer of the company, and said he would be done well before the deadline.

**Canal Office St. Mary's
Sept. 22, 1853**

The excavation and timber work have

been entirely under my control and I am happy to report that both branches are as far advanced as they were expected to be at this time. The delays and difficulties consequent upon doing work 400 miles from source of supplies have been very many and greater than were anticipated. The men have almost all been disabled during the warm weather with a prevailing summer complaint (diarrhea) and been diminished by the efforts of other parties (the iron and copper mines) to hire them away, making it impossible without great exertion to keep a full force of men. But this drawback has been surmounted, the weather has grown cool, the men are healthy and contented and, for the first time in weeks, much greater proportionable progress has been made. I feel safe in promising that everything but the masonry will be finished early next season, extraordinary (problems) excepted. The bulky portion of the wall stone, called backing, I am to see procured and have commenced quarrying 60 miles below here on the river, and the first boat back arrived today.

It will require extraordinary exertion to complete the masonry in time to open the canal, yet I think it *can and will be done.* The number of men employed may be stated in round figures as: excavators, 300; carpenters and helpers, 40; lumbering men, 45; quarry men, 35; (totaling) 420.

The winter proved too cold, the days too short and the rock too hard for Harvey to meet his predictions. The project was taken from him and, although the canal company nearly met financial ruin, the deadline was met. On June 18, 1855, the steamer Illinois became the first ship to sail from Lake Huron to Superior using the two locks. Two months later, the first shipment of iron ore

State Archives, Michigan Dept. of State

Charles Harvey in 1854

passed through for the lower lakes aboard the Baltimore, a steamer that had been pulled across the portage on rollers in 1847. From the James F. Joy papers at the Burton Historical Collection, Detroit Public Library.

1854 *'Some of them are perfect brutes'*

Muscle and fists keep peace on Superior passenger line

Nineteen-year-old George Asa Porter was the new clerk aboard the Sam Ward, one of the few large boats servicing Lake Superior iron and copper mining operations in 1854. In a letter to his mother, he tried to reassure her about life on the big lake.

I believe there is less danger in sailing upon this lake than upon Lake Erie. It is true the seas are heavier and the storms more sudden, but such things as sand bars are unknown and nature has fashioned most of the harbors on a more liberal scale. In a hundred places upon the lake a vessel can run close enough to shore to fasten her lines to the trees. Our engineer especially is a most excellent officer, from his watchfulness, judgment and experience. He has served in the business constantly for nearly 20 years, and during that time is said never to have met with a serious accident to the engines he has had in charge. Capt. Eastabrook is a little too nervous sometimes, but he has had sense enough to choose a first mate of a different stamp. The latter is partly Indian and has been from a child upon Lake Superior. Strange as it may seem to you, most of the deckhands upon the boat are red men. We employ them not only from a scarcity of men, but because they are more *diligent* and patient than others.

Although it is the 7th of June, I find my overcoat quite comfortable, and when we have our *cold* weather, I shall probably be obliged to buy another. The air is very bracing and the country is said to be remarkably healthy. I now weigh a little over 190 pounds. When I come home, I shall easily turn the scale against 200! My stock of clothing is hardly as extensive as it should be, but I think I can work along decently until next winter. I rather expect that when payday comes I shall receive something

Great Lakes Historical Society

The Sam Ward, nearly 176 feet long, was portaged over the St. Mary's River before the Soo Canal was built.

more than $40 per month, but I cannot tell. I receive rather more than enough by taking charge of packages to pay my washing and barber bill. I am fortunate in possessing good bodily strength, for I have had to bring it into play several times. I have had the honor of thrashing two Englishmen without getting injured materially myself.

We carry very heavy loads of passengers and some of them are perfect brutes. When I come across such men and they won't pay their fare, I find it the most expeditious way to hit them a rap. In this way I extricated some change out of a man who, not two days after, came to me making all sorts of apologies and begged my pardon in the humblest manner.

George Porter spent two summers on Lake Superior, then opened a shipping business at Port Huron, serving the Ward shipping line. He came down with a fever on a speaking tour and died at age 23. His niece, May Porter, deposited his letters with the Porter Family papers at the Burton Historical Collection, Detroit Public Library. This letter was submitted by May Porter's distant cousin and friend, Monica Porter of Ferndale.

93

1880s *'We looked like red devils'*

From Escanaba to Cleveland with a cargo of iron ore

As sailors freighted cargoes of iron ore, copper and lumber on the freshwater seas around Michigan in the late 1800s, one of their popular songs was "The Red Iron Ore." The song is a log of the E.C. Roberts' last run of the season, from Chicago to Escanaba, where iron ore is loaded, and on to Cleveland. The Roberts sailed from 1856 until after the turn of the century.

Come listen, young fellows who follow the
   lakes
In iron ore vessels your living to make,
I shipped in Chicago, bid adieu to the shore,
Bound away to Escanaba for red iron ore.
Hi derry! Ho derry! Hi derry, down!
Give sailors good whiskey and they're
   always around.

In the month of September, the 17th day,
Two dollars and a quarter was all they would
   pay;
And on that same day, the North Branch did
   take
The E.C. Roberts out into the lake.

The wind from the sou'west sprang up a stiff
   breeze,
And down through Lake Michigan the
   Roberts did sneeze;
And away through Lake Michigan the
   Roberts did roar;
And on Friday morning we passed through
   death's door.

Across the mouth of Green Bay this packet
   did ride,
With the dark and deep water splashing over
   her side.
We rounded Sand Point and our anchors let
   go,
And we furled all our canvas, and then went
   below.

Next morning we hove 'longside the Exile,
And the Roberts made fast to an iron-ore
   pile.
They let down their chutes and like thunder
   the roar
As they emptied their packets of red iron
   ore.

Some sailors got shovels and others got
   spades,
And more got wheelbarrows — every man to
   his trade.
We looked like red devils, our fingers got
   sore,
And we cursed Escanaba and her red iron
   ore.

The tug Escanaba she towed out the Minch;
The Roberts they thought they had left in a
   pinch;
And as they towed by us they bid us goodby,
Saying, "We'll meet you in Cleveland next
   Fourth of July."

We sailed out alone, through the passage
   steered we,
Passed the Foxes, the Beavers and
   Skilagalee;
We soon passed the Minch for to show her
   the way,
And she never hove in sight till off Thunder
   Bay.

This packet rolled on across Saginaw Bay,
And over her bow there splashed the white
   spray;
And bound for the rivers the Roberts did go,
Where the tug Kate Williams she took us in
   tow.

Now we're in Cleveland, made fast stem and
   stern,
And over the bottle will spin a good yarn.
I think Captain Rumage had ought to stand
   treat
For getting to Cleveland ahead of the fleet.

Institute for Great Lakes Research, Bowling Green State University

The Jessie Martin, a two-masted schooner sailing the Great Lakes at the same time as the E.C. Roberts. It was built at Muskegon in 1881.

The Foxes and Beavers are islands in Northern Lake Michigan and Skilagalee is Isle aux Galets. These verses were recalled by J.S. (Ves) Ray of Port Huron, who learned them from shipmate Billy Clark in the early 1880s. They were collected by Ivan Walton, who spent decades collecting the songs and lore of the Great Lakes. A professor in the University of Michigan's College of Engineering, Walton died in 1968. From the Ivan Walton papers, box eight, in the Michigan Historical Collections at the University of Michigan's Bentley Historical Library.

1873 'Undertakings result in...failure'

Men's unbridled lust for buried riches drives them into the mines

News of Upper Peninsula iron ore deposits began to spread in the 1840s, but even after 30 years and the mining of millions of tons of ore, Marquette Range companies were still going broke. In his Geological Survey of Michigan for 1873, T.B. Brooks described the seductive lure of dreams of sudden wealth.

The history of the development of a good many of our iron mining enterprises has been somewhat as follows: The deposit is found, sometimes by accident, but often by systematic explorations. A boulder of ore, red soil in the roots of a fallen tree, the variation of the magnetic needle, the proximity of rocks supposed to belong to the iron range, and often the outcrop of the ore itself determine where digging shall be commenced.

If the indications are promising, before many marks are made the land is secured. If government land, it is "entered" at the land office at $1.25 per acre, or $2.50 if within the limits of some railroad grant.

Our supposed exploring party, having secured the land, begin to dig test pits and trenches openly and systematically.

Specimens, which I am sorry to say are apt to be the best that can be found, are sent in as *averages* of the deposit. Experts pronounce them shipping ore and common talk asserts that so-and-so have a "good show" for a mine.

Next in order, some prominent man of character and means is found to take the presidency of the company, his friends, with others, being "let in" on the "ground floor," and the None-such Iron Co. is organized and at work.

A contract is usually let to some French Canadian to build a dozen log homes for miners' families, a company's store, barn and shop. In clearing for the foundations, it is usual for the Frenchman to find a new deposit of ore better than the one first found, to which a part of the mining force is at once transferred, the location of the building being changed so as to avoid the fragments which blasting has already begun to throw.

About this time the president of the company and a part of the board of directors visit the mine. One of the directors is an eminent lawyer who helped to "place" the property, another is a stockbroker who had made a fortune in Wall Street, a third is a railroad king and another a successful whisky distiller. None but the president knew anything of iron before they came into the company.

Having spent one half-day in the examination of their property, and becoming satisfied that it is first-class and will prove a profitable investment for themselves and friends, the company leave, having first instructed their superintendent to bend all his energies to getting out ore, without reference to quality, cost or future condition of the mine — though the whole is not, of course, directly expressed.

The foregoing sketch contains the elements on which many Lake Superior iron mining enterprises have been organized, and at the start operated. It is needless to remark that many such undertakings result in utter failure. In the copper region the proportion of failures is far greater, and in oil, gold, and silver enterprises overwhelmingly so. The average human imagination becomes temporarily diseased when stimulated by the chances of possessing hidden mineral wealth. Iron, being the least valuable of the metals, has less of this influence than the others, but it is not entirely free from it.

From "Geological Survey of Michigan for 1869-1873," published by the Michigan Legislature in New York, 1873: pages 187-190.

Free Press files

The Jackson Mine being worked with horses, buckets and wagons.

From ''Geological Survey of
Michigan for 1869-1873.''

Looking west in the Jackson
Mine's No. 1 pit, as depicted
by an artist.

1878 *'Great times getting in logs'*

Farmer spends the winter measuring green gold

Joseph Proctor, 42, a farmer at Hersey in Osceola County, spent the winter of 1877-78 as a "scaler," estimating the amount of lumber cut at logging camps near Cadillac. His letters described how dependent the camps were on the ice and snow that let them skid logs out of the woods to the riverbank. There the "green gold" was piled on high "rollways" to await the spring river drive.

Maxim's Camp, Jan. 9

We have had some cold weather but the snow is only about three inches deep. They are drawing logs with what teams they have, but the teams are not all here yet. They have stopped cutting timber and I am not hurried much now.

Maxim's Camp, Jan. 16

Snow is only about two inches deep. They have to carry and draw snow quite a distance to keep their road up. But they draw big loads.

Jan. 29

The other scaler has gone home and I have to do one day's scaling at Ducheney's camp each week. My work is not very hard now but hard enough to suit me.

Feb. 20, Camp No. 3

We are having great times getting in logs here. One day will be light snow, then it will thaw. Today was a bad one for us. I thought that we should get snow last night, but it turned around in the night and rained some, then froze towards morning, so we done a very good forenoon's work, but the sun came out so hot in the afternoon that we lost nearly all of our snow. Some of our roads are all mud.

Feb. 27, Camp No. 3

This kind of business I do not like. We are working night and day and I do not get much rest. It is now between 2 and 3 o'clock in the morning. I have been to bed and slept about two hours, but I shall soon be in bed again. I have had the oxen out drawing snow (to cover the logging roads) and now have just came in from sending the horse teams out.

We have not stopped drawing but for two days since I came up (Feb. 12), and that was when it rained.

March 7

We can't draw any more logs unless there is a big change in the weather. I shall be at home about the 25th of this month if I can possibly get away.

We are looking about to see if we can break rollways. Blodgett (the camp owner) wants me to stay with the men, but I shan't do any rollway breaking myself. I have not time to write much this time, but will write in full next time. It is all excitement here now.

March 9

The excitement is pretty much over. My men are over half gone so I can rest again. I send the ox teams all away today, but three, which we will keep here to break the rollways.

A year earlier, a narrow-gauge railroad had been built in a state forest. With encouragement from Proctor and other loggers, the railroads spread and the logging industry became less reliant on snow to get logs to the mills. Michigan lumber production hit its peak in 1888 and led the nation for the rest of the century. Proctor's great-granddaughter, Jean Proctor Chase of Northville, says he lived into his 90s. His diaries were donated to the Michigan Historical Collections at the University of Michigan's Bentley Historical Library after his death.

State Archives, Michigan Dept. of State

Two loggers ham it up in a Michigan logging camp. Loggers used poles with hinged hooks at one end to maneuver logs. Long poles with a spike on the hook end were called peaveys, shorter tools without spikes were cant hooks.

1880s *'The winter of the blue snow'*

Paul Bunyan stands tall in the logging camps

In camps from Atlantic to Pacific, loggers working in the late 1800s spun yarns about the greatest lumberman ever, Paul Bunyan. Nowhere was the legend richer than in Michigan, but some of the "shanty boys" were given to exaggeration. Leon May, "the camp cook from Fife Lake," sets the record straight.

There have been so many so-called tall tales of the Paul Bunyan camps that it seems to me it is about time that someone straightened out some of the facts about the camp and told those facts as they really are.

You see, I was born not far from Old Paul's camp on the Tobacco River. Kinda funny how that river got its name. 'Twas just a little crick when Old Paul set up his camp there. Mighty fine cold water. Old Paul figured it would be just right for the cook to use and the boys to drink. Well, sir, that winter the boys sat around the camp an awful lot because of heavy snow, and setting around there they chawed an awful lot of tobacco. Old Paul always treated his help right, and he issued a pound of plug to each man each morning. Well, sir, setting around the camp they chawed and spit and spit and chawed, all the time spitting out the window. When it thawed out in the spring, instead of that crick being nice and clear, it was brown with tobacco juice. From that time till now it has been called Tobacco River. And do you know that was where they first started catching brown trout in Michigan?

Well, as I said, I was raised near there, and when Old Paul moved his camp over by Houghton Lake, I was pretty lonesome. I made up my mind that as soon as I got growed up I'd go up there to work.

The first job I did for Paul was to help him build a rain barrel. That must have been the biggest rain barrel that ever was built. It held 989 barrels, 28 gallons, one quart, one-half pint, one gill and three tablespoons full, lacking eight drops. I know that's right because I measured it carefully.

That was the winter of the blue snow, the coldest winter Michigan ever knew. It got down to 73¼ degrees below zero, and every degree was a foot long. It was so cold that it took me two days and nine minutes to light a match on a steam grindstone. It got so cold that it froze the flames in the lamps and we couldn't blow them out. So we just broke off the flames and threw them out of the windows. Most of them we threw out. But when we ran out of pepper, the cook ground some of them up for seasoning. When spring came, those flames thawed out and started a fire in the woods. That fire ran clean to St. Mary's River and burned it in two. Of course, this held up navigation and made the water back up in Lake Superior so that the folks up at Duluth wrote Old Paul and asked him what he was going to do about it.

So the next morning Old Paul took one of the wagon boxes off a wagon and a shovel and went up there and put that wagon box in where the river was burned in two. That was the first ship canal at the Soo. It was quite a job, and Old Paul was 18 minutes late for dinner.

Now these are some facts about Paul Bunyan's camp. I could tell you some real whoppers about Old Paul, but you must remember that I am trying to sort out the truths.

From Earl Clifton Beck's "They Knew Paul Bunyan," University of Michigan Press, Ann Arbor, 1956: pages 4-11.

Mead Corp., Dayton, Ohio

Paul Bunyan and Babe, the blue ox, yank the Round River straight with a huge pair of ice tongs.

1885 *'Ten hours or no sawdust'*

Strike for shorter days shuts Saginaw mills

A strike shut sawmills up and down the Saginaw Valley in 1885 and raised tensions to a fever pitch. Before the strike, men had worked about 11 hours a day, six days a week, for an average $1.70 a day. They struck for 10-hour workdays at the same pay. Gov. Russell Alger, who made his fortune in lumber, sent Labor Commissioner Cornelius Pond to investigate. These excerpts are from Pond's July 23 report.

I reached Saginaw on Thursday the 16th, and found with one or two exceptions all the lumber and shingle mills and salt blocks on the Saginaw River were closed and the employes idle. (Scraps from the mills were burned to evaporate water from brine to produce salt.) The number of industries closed aggregated 120 and covered a distance of 20 miles along the river in the counties of Saginaw and Bay. The number of persons thrown out of employment was variously estimated at from 6,000 to 7,000.

There can be no doubt in my mind, after conversing with hundreds of men singly or in groups of not over seven, that employes of the Saginaw Valley, having heard that the Legislature had recently passed a law making 10 hours a legal day's work, supposed that the law took effect July 1st instead of Sept. 19, as is the fact.

The mills, as is customary, had closed for the legal holiday Fourth of July, and without doubt any who were given to excess of drink did discuss the question of hours of labor.

The hours of labor to the time of shutting down among the industries affected by the strike were 11 to 11¼ and 11½, the 11-hour system prevailing. The men get to work at 6 o'clock in the morning and continue until noon, resume at 1 o'clock and work until 6.

The strike really occurred Monday forenoon July 6, when a few men from W.B. Rouse's Mill about two miles below Bay City — closed for cleaning of boilers — were passing McEwan Bros. and Leo's Mill — closed because of lack of presence of entire crew. One of the Rouse crew took out a red handkerchief, put it upon a stick and shouted, "Hurrah for 10 hours" — this the man said he did in fun. The cry was at once taken up and, under the lead of three men who had not been working this season, a force of 100 men proceeded up the river, where they were met by Sheriff Brennan and told they must not interfere with the workingmen. The next mill visited was that of Pitts & Cranage, but the workingmen would not quit work. The cry was now, "Ten hours or no sawdust."

To keep order, Gov. Alger sent in the state militia and businesses hired 150 Pinkerton guards. It was the first of several strikes in which Michigan troops and private guards would be used. The strike, led by the Knights of Labor, ended when the 10-hour law took effect in September. Pond's report is in the Michigan State Archives in Lansing.

Bay County Historical Society

Workers and children posed with a saw blade at the Hitchcock & Bialy Mill in Bay City, 1882. The barrels on the roof held water, in case of fire.

Delta County Historical Society

Capt. Soren Kristiansen with cook John Frazer, left, and engineer Charles Girari, right.

1891 *'The first vessel to that tannery'*

Lake Michigan bark trade keeps schooner moving

Soren Kristiansen, a native of Norway, began sailing on the Great Lakes in 1886 and, in 1891, was working on a schooner ferrying bark across Lake Michigan to Wisconsin tanneries. His diary shows a job that was far from glamorous and meant a lot of waiting for cargo, for tows and for better weather.

Monday, June 1

I got to Sheboygan (Wis.) last night with a hold full of wood and a deck load of bark on the scow Mishicoff. I towed up the river with the tug Fred Nielson to C.T. Roenets Tannery. There I unloaded and measured out 44 cords of bark and 27 ⅛ cords of wood. Mishicoff was the first vessel to that tannery this year and it was slow unloading, but they promised better dispatch later on when they got things in shape.

In Onekama (Mich.), Tuesday, June 9

We started to load in the morning with bark. We are loading from the R.R. cars. We are putting a slide from the cars down on the vessel and the men on the cars is putting the bark in the slide and it slides right down on the vessel, where there is men to take care of it and stow it away. It is very laborious work, especially if it is very dry. It then breaks up and makes a very slow work of it. It costs from $6 to $10 a cord, according to the quality needed in the market.

Arrival at Onekama, Tuesday, June 30

The schooner Vermont came along the shore and we both sailed for the Portage Lake piers, which we made about 1 o'clock in the afternoon. We both sailed in and made fast to R.R. pier. Nothing more was done that day because we had no bark.

In Onekama, Wednesday, July 1

In the morning we had two carloads of bark and we started to work with a whole lot of boys from 12 to 15 years of age and we got them two carloads in and laid around the rest of the day waiting for bark.

In Onekama, Thursday, July 2

We took in all the bark we had on the R.R. pier and at 4 o'clock in the afternoon we towed to Schroeder's pier and finished off our load. It came up with a squall from the NW, and we made her fast for the night.

Leaving Onekama, Friday, July 3

About 6 o'clock in the morning we gave her the canvas and sailed from Schroeder's pier down the lake to meet the tug Wallace, who towed out the Vermont and the Madonna. He met us about halfway between the piers and Onekama and we handed him the line. He took us out to lake. It was a good breeze from NW, which hauled to the westward all the time and the Mishicoff started to leak so that we could hardly keep her clear. So the captain made up his mind to go for Ludington.

In Ludington, Saturday, July 4

The wind is NW, strong and clear. This is the day of freedom for the United States and it is celebrated in a very large scale at many places in the country. I was sitting on the deck load for a while and looking at all the rockets and fireworks in town, and when I thought I had seen enough I went to bed.

In 1893, Kristiansen began a 20-year tour of duty as master of the lightship 11-Foot Shoal, anchored near Escanaba. He then became lighthouse keeper at Escanaba, retiring in 1925 at age 70. He died in 1932. The diary was given to the Delta County Historical Society by Robert Jensen of Escanaba, whose family knew Kristiansen. It was published by the Mid-Peninsula Library Co-operative, Iron Mountain, in 1981.

1909 '1,500 tons of ore at a mine a day'

Young Swede jokes about having iron mine's highest position

Not yet 20, George Erickson had a job on a platform where iron ore was brought up out of a mine in the western Upper Peninsula. He wrote frequently to his boyhood friend, Linus Paulin, back home in Jarnboas, Sweden. Erickson's letters describe life around the time "Mutt and Jeff" were funny-paper favorites and the top tunes included "Let Me Call You Sweetheart."

Dec. 12, 1909

I have soon been in this country three months and I like it here in Stambaugh. I work at a mine now. I have been here at it for two weeks. I work on the landing. I have to shovel all the ore and gray dirt that comes up out of the mine. It's good work, even though it is cold, but now they have a little house that we can crawl into when we have a minute. We get $2.15 a day, and on that you can get along. You don't have to pay more than $18 a month for food, so if you want to save, you usually have a few dollars left over.

Jan. 10, 1910

Here in America you don't have to go without work if you want to do something. I never had to look for work. I got it anyway. So there is certainly a difference between here and Sweden, where you have to bow and be humble and ask everywhere and still don't get any work anyway.

I have it quite good here — no danger to life since I don't work underground. Instead I am high up in the air and work on the landing, so I can say that I have the highest position in the company!

I can also tell you, to show how anxious the Americans are to work, that we worked on Christmas Eve, but we quit at 3:30, so that was liberal. We were free New Year's Day also, but now it will just be work until the Fourth of July, when we will get a day off

again, so they don't have many holidays in America.

March 3, 1910

People here don't have any more energy than people in Sweden, although everything goes faster here because everything is done by machinery. For example, they take up 1,500 tons of ore at a mine a day. The ore is never more than 65 percent but is used anyway.

May 22, 1910

I begin work at 7 a.m., have 1½ hours for dinner, and quit at 5 p.m. I'm sending a picture of some gentlemen. (One man) is from Ireland. He got fired one day because he hit the boss on the head with a sledgehammer.

June, 1910

You ask if I have seen any airships yet. I have not, to tell the truth, but there are so many automobiles. They drive with them wherever they go. Soon you can't walk on the roads because of these crazy things.

Dec. 26, 1910

If you aren't born here you can't get in with folks the way you would like. You know that those who are born here believe they are better than those who come from another country.

April 11, 1911

Today is election day in Stambaugh so you can be sure things are lively. There is a terrible fuss over politics here in America, and nothing is too low to make use of. The big mining companies are doing everything they can to get their man in. They offer people free beer, liquor and cigars to get people on their side. There probably isn't a country in the world that has as much graft as America. When they work so hard in a

Courtesy Martha Johnson

George Erickson and Edla Lindblom on their wedding day on May 11, 1916.

small place like this, what wouldn't they do in larger places?

After returning to Michigan from a visit home in 1914, Erickson wrote:

You can imagine how hard it was to leave again, but I also thought it was good to get away from all oppression and all that I would have to do if I stayed in Sweden. Here you are, in any event, a free man in a free country.

Erickson became an American citizen and married Edla Lindblom, another Swedish immigrant, in 1916. He died in 1950. The letters were translated by his oldest daughter, Martha Johnson of Chicago, and many, including these, were reprinted in "Letters to Linus," The Swedish Pioneer Historical Quarterly (October, 1974): pages 231-246.

Car capital

"There is a saying that you can stand in the Place de l'Opera in Paris and, if you stay there a while, the whole world will pass by. You can stand in a square of Detroit and the entire automobile business of the world will pass by, and you won't have to stand there very long, either."
— Hugh Chalmers

1897 *'Ford seems to have difficulties'*

His engines are fine for boats, but can they propel buggies?

Henry Ford drove his first horseless carriage through the streets of Detroit in 1896 and, in 1897, a small group of investors watched his progress closely. One backer, former city comptroller Ellery I. Garfield, was interested, but cautious, and expressed his concerns in this Sept. 21, 1897, letter to William Maybury, Detroit mayor and a Ford family friend.

My Dear Maybury:

I note what you say of the motor wagon and your conclusions with regard to it. I do not wonder that you are somewhat discouraged, as I am, for Mr. Ford seems to have difficulties as well as all the others. I think I said to you in one of my former letters that I believed one of the greatest drawbacks in motor wagons to be that they are all trying to see how light a wagon they can make.

I have been doing a great deal of thinking, and the result is I have in mind a very serious doubt as to whether gasoline engines are the proper thing for motor carriages; or for that matter any power that is produced by explosion.

Take, for instance, a carriage that is standing still, no matter whether it is a buggy or express wagon, and suppose that a slight obstruction is directly in the way of the front wheel. In case of gasoline or any other explosive, a certain kick is made by the explosion and there is no further explosion until the carriage has moved a certain distance, which, of course, is very short. The force of the kick is all you obtain. It is not a continued pressure, as is the case of steam or electricity.

In the case of anything explosive, it comes with a rush for an instant only and then all is gone. This, of course, must be a great strain on a light wagon or light machinery. This is where, I think, we in this country have made a great mistake; in trying to build too-light engines and wagons.

I can readily see how some of the engines Mr. Ford has made have been sold for small boats and work very well. When they are on a boat and in the water and the explosion is made, the propeller of course will continue to turn as there is not a great amount of resistance.

Your letter is dated the 16th, and Mr. Ford's promise to you of 30 days would make it about the middle of October. I sincerely trust he will have something that will be a long way ahead of any carriage at that time. If it is practical and he can overcome the difficulties that have been in the way of all others, he will have something that is valuable, and of which he can take hold and make money.

Despite his misgivings, Garfield joined Maybury, Ford and several other businessmen to form the Detroit Automobile Co. in 1899. Ford produced virtually nothing and had serious disagreements with his backers. In 1901, he left the company and, in 1903, he and others created Ford Motor Co. It built its 20 millionth car in 1931. From the William C. Maybury papers, 1896-1897, in the Burton Historical Collection, Detroit Public Library.

Collections of Henry Ford Museum and Greenfield Village

Henry Ford at the tiller of his first car, a buggy chassis mounted on four bicycle wheels and powered by a two-cylinder gasoline engine, in 1896.

1902 *'Great to ... travel in electrics'*

Horatio 'Good Roads' Earle paves way for highways

Automobiles were still an oddity in 1902, but there was a strong movement for better roads — championed by bicyclists. In Michigan, the campaign was led by Horatio 'Good Roads' Earle, a former foundry apprentice and farm tool salesman. His trademark was the Good Roads Train, a string of as many as 40 wagons hauled over dirt roads by a traction engine. Earle used the train to take people to rallies, where he demonstrated the latest methods in road building. As Earle tried to win support, he made these entries in his diary.

May 5

Mr. J.H. Simpson, assistant general manager of the Pere Marquette Railway System, has granted my request for a Good Roads Train free of charge to be hauled over their line anywhere I desire. Who would have thought an iron molder from (Chicopee, Mass.) would have had such an amount of influence?

May 14

Am going to have all I can do with road work this summer.

June 4

Spoke at State Horticultural Mid-Summer Meeting at Pontiac on good roads. It is great to be able to travel in electrics (streetcars) 26 miles and back again in one afternoon and have time to attend a meeting besides.

July 1

Railroads have granted me half-fare rates to Michigan Good Roads Exposition at Greenville. I couldn't have got this two years ago.

July 29

Am at Hotel Phelps, Greenville, Mich. More people here today than came to Port

State Archives, Michigan Dept. of State
Horatio S. Earle, father of the good roads movement in Michigan.

Huron International Good Roads Congress (in 1900) in four days. I hope for a crowd tomorrow.

(Road-building) machinery was set to work only yesterday, but they have done mighty well.

July 30

Good judges say we had 15,000 people here today. And it is already the most successful good roads meeting ever held in the United States.

My Good Roads Train drew a thousand

State Archives, Michigan Dept. of State

One of the Good Roads trains used to take people to exhibitions of modern road-building techniques.

people to the grounds and it was a success, and I feel well paid for being tired.

July 31

At Dexter Hotel, Ionia, Mich. Had 8,000 people today, making 24,000 in three days.

Gov. (Aaron) Bliss came; I took him to a ball game, and at 4:30 he spoke from stand and made the best speech I ever heard him make. Mayor E.P. Lapham of Belding and others and myself spoke, and thus ended the most successful good roads meeting I ever attended, and I am proud of having had a part in the promotion of it.

Earle became Michigan's first highway commissioner and, in 1909, while he held office, the world's first mile of concrete paving was laid on Woodward Avenue between Six and Seven Mile Roads. The highway construction boom that followed eventually put some of Earle's supporters — the railroads — out of business. Earle's diaries are in the Michigan Historical Collections at the University of Michigan's Bentley Historical Library.

113

The industrial development on Flint's north side in 1909. Imperial Wheel is just to the right of center, behind the low building on the river.

1906 *'Abide by the following'*

Plant rules ban profanity, smoking and undignified talking

In 1906, Flint workers were required to sign a contract before starting work at Imperial Wheel Co. The company, one of many linked to the young auto industry, was affiliated with Durant-Dort Carriage Co., which built horse-drawn carriages. Most of the contract's provisions are excerpted here.

Please do not accept employment unless you are willing to abide by the following regulations.

WORKING HOURS — 6:30 a.m. to 11:30 a.m. standard time; 12:30 p.m. to 5:30 p.m. standard time, except on Saturday when the day ends at 4:30 standard time. First whistle blows at five minutes before the beginning of working hours. Second whistle on working hours. Overtime 6 p.m. to 9 p.m.

Employes shall be in their respective departments prepared to begin work when second whistle blows, and if frequently or habitually late may expect dismissal.

Employes will remain at their work until the whistle blows, and *all changing of clothing, washing or cleaning up will be done after working hours.*

Billy Durant, left, and J. Dallas Dort confer outside Imperial Wheel in 1908.

Photos courtesy the Flint Journal

An interior view of the Imperial Wheel Co.

SMOKING in any building or about the yards is not allowed except in the Boiler Room, and not there during working hours.

All bicycles, clothing, shoes, etc., must be kept in places provided for that purpose in each department.

All persons, except those authorized, are strictly forbidden to use elevators and then for freighting purposes only, and all employes are warned against meddling with electric motors or any electrical appliances in any way, save as authorized by their foremen.

Each employe will attend strictly to his own work, and no one will permit himself to indulge in any loud talking, profanity or undignified talking during working hours.

SUBSCRIPTION PAPERS. The passing of subscription papers through the factory in the interest of disabled employes will not be encouraged for the reason that every employe may protect himself against such a necessity by becoming a member of some association, which will provide for the payment to him weekly of a given sum of money in case of sickness, accident or death.

Imperial Wheel Co. had been lured to Flint from Jackson by the city's promise of a free factory site. The coup nearly cost Flint a larger prize, Buick Motor Car Co. In 1904, Billy Durant, of Durant-Dort Co., became a director of Buick and moved its assembly operations from Flint into the vacant Imperial works in Jackson. Flint bankers persuaded him to bring Buick back by buying $100,000 in stock. From the John J. Carton papers in the Michigan Historical Collections at the University of Michigan's Bentley Historical Library.

Zeeland Historical Society

This was the main street of Zeeland around the turn of the century.

1907 *'Our history reads like fiction'*

Electric lights and the telephone: Who would have believed it?

Things changed considerably in the 60 years after the Rev. Albertus C. Van Raalte founded a Dutch colony in western Michigan in 1847. For the 1907 anniversary celebration, the Rev. D. R. Drukker marveled at the changes, contrasting the conditions of six decades previous with the comforts of his modern age.

What a change. Our history reads like fiction. Yet is true. Look at the place of our habitation. Sixty years ago our fathers found Ottawa and north Allegan Counties a howling wilderness.

Now mark the change. The forests, to our sorrow, are all gone. The whole has been transformed into well-cultivated farms upon which you find beautiful homes. Low lands are drained and cultivated, the old log, stump, yea, rail fence is a thing of the past, and wire fences — as advertised — "horse high, bull strong, pig tight" now parcel off the farms.

Then our fathers went to the house of God afoot, now our churchyards resemble a huge livery stable on the Sabbath day; carriages of every description, of the latest model and of the best quality are found in great numbers. Even the horseless wagon — concerning which a man once made the following statement: "The only thing I like of those benzene buggies is the smell, for then danger is past" — the same has invaded our colony and goes wheezing through our cities and villages.

Our fathers made the forests to resound with their "Whoa!" and "Gee!" and the sons drive an automobile.

Let us, as sons, be careful not to purchase an automobile on wheelbarrow wages.

Here is the development with regard to travel: afoot, ox-team lumber wagon, platform wagon, top buggy, surrey, bicycle, electric car, automobile — what next?

Today, our homes are mansions, they vie with the best in the land. Our furniture suitable for a governor's home, of the best material, expensive, and many have not paid for theirs. Our walls are decorated by the artists' skill; in nearly every home of our progressive Holland America you will find a library. Our beds are so soft we are loath to get up in the morning. Gas and electricity cook our meals and illumine our homes; the hard-coal stoves and furnaces make our homes comfortable in zero weather. We eat and drink of what is found on the king's table, we hardly know what to eat at times; we dress in the latest styles and use the best material. The wooden shoe has been exchanged for the patent leather; the blue overall for broadcloth, the calico dress for silk. The primitive headgear of our mothers and sisters exchanged for a piece of bent-up straw as if drawn through a wringer, adorned with red, white and blue.

Compare the old cornstalk stack and the silo, the milkpan and the separator, the churn and the creamery; the old-time foot messenger and the telephone, binding the colony together, erasing distances and promoting the pleasures of life; the mail carrier, who visits us once, twice or three times a week with the rural delivery of today.

The community founded by Mr. Van Raalte is Holland. Drukker's address was written for a celebration at Zeeland on Aug. 21, 1907. From "Historical Souvenir of the Celebration of the 60th Anniversary of the Colonization of Hollanders in Western Michigan," Zeeland, 1908: pages 27-31.

1910 *'Detroit produces any kind of car'*

Predictions of a long, competitive future for the automobile industry

The automobile had turned Detroit into a booming town by 1910, the year the city held its first auto show. But how long would the auto manufacturing boom last? Hugh Chalmers, 36, president of the Detroit-Chalmers Motor Co., made these observations in an address at Detroit College, now the University of Detroit.

The automobile business has been built up so rapidly, and particularly in Detroit, that the people of Detroit generally do not realize what the automobile industry means.

In order to realize what a tremendous industry it is, and how Detroit is affected by it, it is necessary for me to give you some facts and some figures:

It is estimated that there are 150 automobile companies in the United States. There are 35 companies in Michigan, with a total capacity of 140,000 cars annually; 23 of these 35 companies are in Detroit, with a total annual output of 85,000 cars and a total capitalization of $30 million.

There are 39,000 people employed by automobile manufacturers in Detroit, and 19,000 employed by accessory manufacturers.

Detroit formerly was proud of the fact that it made more stoves, more pills, more paint and more freight cars than any other city in the country. The volume of the largest of these products in dollars and cents — freight cars — amounts to about $18 million annually. The product of any two of the more prominent automobile companies in Detroit will easily total $20 million a year.

Detroit produces any kind of car that anyone can want, from a $500 runabout to an $8,000 limousine.

There is a saying that you can stand in the Place de l'Opera in Paris and, if you stay there a while, the whole world will pass by.

You can stand in a square of Detroit and the entire automobile business of the world will pass by, and you won't have to stand there very long, either.

People naturally ask, "How long will the automobile business continue and isn't it likely to be overdone?" Now, I am not a prophet and cannot tell just what is going to happen, but I believe the automobile is not subject to any other comparison, because the automobile is the first improvement in individual transportation in centuries. I think the automobile will be with us as long as the horse has been with us. But whether or not the public can take the output of some 200 automobile companies is another question.

I believe that the automobile business will be the leading industry of Detroit for more years yet than any of us will live and I am not so fearful of a reaction in the present situation, because there are so many companies that are building good cars located here. Of course, many people figure that where money has been made, it still can be made, and the danger ahead of us is that too many people will get to thinking that way. Personally, I would not take too much stock in any new company that was just starting, because I believe the competition in the future is going to be keener by far than it has been in the past, and competition, of course, means the elimination of those who are unable to withstand it.

Chalmers died in 1932 in New York after catching pneumonia while on an automobile tour. He is credited with bringing modern merchandising techniques to the auto industry. His speech was reprinted in the April 23, 1910, issue of Automobile Topics, pages 136-138.

Free Press Files

Detroit's first auto show in 1910 — when steering wheels were still on the righthand side.

A sea of faces, all looking for work at $5 a day.

<u>1914</u> *'The greatest revolution'*

Ford stuns business world with the $5 day

Reporters for the Detroit Free Press, Detroit News and Detroit Journal were called to Ford Motor Co. offices in Highland Park on the morning of Jan. 5, 1914, for an announcement. With most of the world in a recession, the company had been a rare bright spot. Its Model T was selling so well that on Aug. 1, 1913, the price had been cut for the fourth time in three years. Workers had received 13 percent raises on Oct. 1, but still had wages that were typical for the industry — less than 30 cents an hour for a nine-hour day. The reporters were called into the office of Vice-President James Couzens, who read two typed sheets of paper as Henry Ford stood near a window.

The Ford Motor Co., the greatest and most successful automobile manufacturing company in the world, will, on Jan. 12, inaugurate the greatest revolution in the matter of rewards for its workers ever known to the industrial world.

At one stroke it will reduce the hours of labor from nine to eight, and add to every man's pay a share of the profits of the house. The smallest amount to be received by any man 22 years old and upwards will be $5 per day. The minimum wage is now $2.34 per day of nine hours.

All but 10 percent of the employes will at once share in the profits. Only 10 percent of the men now employed are now under 22 and even every one of those under 22 will have a chance of showing himself entitled to $5 per day.

Instead of waiting until the end of the year to make a distribution of profits among their employes in one lump sum, Mr. Ford and Mr. Couzens have estimated the year's prospective business and have decided upon what they feel will be a safe amount to award the workers. This will be spread over the whole year and paid on the regular semimonthly paydays.

The factory is now working two shifts of nine hours each. This will be changed to

Collections of Henry Ford Museum and Greenfield Village

Ten thousand applicants mobbed the Ford employment office the day after new jobs were announced.

three shifts of eight hours each. The number employed is now about 15,000 and this will be increased by 4,000 or 5,000. The men who now earn $2.34 per day of nine hours will get at least $5 per day of eight hours.

This will apply to every man of 22 years of age or upward without regard to the nature of his employment. In order that the young man, from 18 to 22 years of age, may be entitled to a share in the profits, he must show himself sober, saving, steady, industrious, and must satisfy the superintendent and staff that his money will not be wasted in riotous living.

Young men who are supporting families, widowed mothers, younger brothers and sisters, will be treated like those over 22.

It is estimated that over $10 million will be thus distributed over and above the regular wages of men.

Without litigation, legislation or negotiation, Ford Motor Co. more than doubled the standard wage for the industry. The $5 day struck the business community like a thunderbolt and was front-page news in newspapers around the world. At 7:30 the next morning, 10,000 men mobbed the Ford employment office. The industry was slow to adopt the $5 day, and Ford itself did not extend it to women for almost two years, but eight-hour days quickly became the norm. From Harry Barnard, "Independent Man: The Life of Sen. James Couzens," Charles Scribner's Sons, New York, 1958: pages 91-93.

1915 'We believe in the automobile'

So many farmers buy cars bank asks Ford for money

Henry Ford grew up on a farm and worked to make sure his automobile was a machine every farmer would want and could afford. He cut prices to less than $500 on some models and the Ford became known as the farmer's car. For some people, though, the car was too popular with farmers. J. Jones, head cashier at the tiny Manton State Bank north of Cadillac, wrote on June 12, 1915, to tell Henry Ford how the car's success was hurting his bank.

Dear Sir:

This bank is now confronted with a problem which it has never faced before, which seems to us to be brought about by the automobile situation. This is a strictly farming community and our business is almost entirely with farmers. The country is quite new, only partially cleared, and many farmers (are) on new farms with little cleared land and are poor and have to have help at seeding time and while they are raising crops. It is our business to take deposits from farmers that have the older farms who have some money ahead and loan it to those that need the help. But now the older farmers are drawing their money out to buy automobiles to such an extent that we find we are unable to get the usual amount of deposits with which to accommodate our customers. We are now loaned up to our legal reserve and there are still a great many farmers that we cannot accommodate as we have been in the habit of doing. If our farmers cannot get help, they cannot put in the crops and make the improvements on their farms that they should and would if we had the money to loan them.

Our bank pays three percent on money deposited three months, and 3½ percent if left one year. If we could have a deposit of from $5,000 to $10,000 from your company, we could loan it at good advantage and could

Averaging about two cents a mile in daily use, Ford cars are a necessity to every business man, doctor, salesman or farmer. And they serve the family just as well. Every man is his own mechanic with a Ford. No need of high-priced experts. And "Ford After-Service for Ford Owners" is a good thing to remember.

Buyers will share in profits if we sell at retail 300,000 new Ford cars between August 1914 and August 1915.

Runabout $440; Touring Car $490; Town Car $690; Coupelet $750; Sedan $975, f. o. b. Detroit with all equipment.

On display and sale at Ford Motor Co., 1550 Woodward Ave.

This 1915 ad told farmers that a Ford car was a necessity and could be purchased for as little as $440.

pay it back to you in six months with interest. The automobile has taken out at least $10,000 from our deposits, which would be here to loan but for it. We believe in the automobile and are glad to see the people enjoying them and to see the improved road conditions brought about by the auto.

Three days later, Ford Motor Co.'s H.S. Morgan responded:

We have your letter of the 12th, and while we appreciate all you have done to assist in the promotion of the automobile business in your particular territory, we beg to advise that this company is not now opening any

Collections of Henry Ford Museum and Greenfield Village

A Ford truck, loaded with hay in 1921.

new accounts, although we have no doubt but that a connection with your bank would prove mutually satisfactory were it possible for us to deposit any funds with you. Owing to the uncertainty as to the amount of funds required in the event of our profit-sharing with our retail purchasers, however, we discontinued opening any new accounts some time ago.

From letters submitted by Millie Flanagan of the Manton Area Historical Museum.

1925 *'To yield maximum mileage'*

Car engineer makes plans for oil shortage

In the fall of 1925, Charles Kettering, the engineering genius at General Motors Corp., sounded a warning: Oil won't last forever. He told the American Chemical Society that the auto industry must plan for shortages to come.

The past two decades have seen the most remarkable development in transportation ever witnessed in the world's history. This development is the almost universal use of the automobile by the American public. Enormous quantities of motor fuel are being consumed by these automobiles.

Though there appears to be no immediate danger of our subterranean tanks of petroleum running dry, it is evident that every gallon of petroleum taken out of the ground leaves one gallon less to be taken out of the ground in the future, and some day — no one knows just when — our petroleum reserves will have diminished to the point where we can no longer supply our motorists with a quantity of cheap, volatile motor fuel from this source.

No economically satisfactory substitute is immediately available. Many years of research may be necessary before the actual development of such a substitute can start. More years of development may be necessary before practical results of a quantitative nature are obtained. If a petroleum shortage should occur during these years, the enormous utility of automotive transportation would be seriously hampered. Such a catastrophe can be largely avoided, or at least greatly modified, if motorcar fuel economy can be materially increased.

The factors affecting miles per gallon are so diverse and so interrelated that in order to obtain a comprehensive picture of the whole it will be well mentally to construct an automobile to yield maximum mileage.

This hypothetical car will have the following characteristics:

• It will be very small, with narrow tread and short wheelbase.

• It will be very light, made of the best materials for strength obtainable.

• It will look rather odd, being streamlined throughout to reduce windage, and it will have no top, windshield or mudguards.

• It will have a conventional but small radiator.

• It will have a small, high-compression motor, adjusted to run on gasoline treated with an anti-knock material.

• The carburetor will be quite complex; practically no one but the designer will be able to adjust it.

• The ignition system will be complicated to such an extent that the spark advance will always be correct for each speed and load.

• The transmission will have four speeds forward and one reverse, so designed that when in high gear all other gears will be disconnected.

• The rear axle will be so geared that only on the level can the motor pull the car with the high gear.

• The brakes will be carefully made and adjusted so that when not in use they are entirely free of any contact with the wheels.

Until some practical invention of great merit makes its appearance, the above are probably the most hopeful design possibilities for economy.

Kettering's views were presented in the 1925 symposium on Motor Fuel and Oil Conservation at the International Meeting of the American Chemical Society in New York City. From the November, 1925, issue of Industrial and Engineering Chemistry, pages 1,115 and 1,116.

Detroit Free Press files

Charles Kettering works with one of his innovations, the electric self-starter.

Citizens
of the world

"Far better that our sons should die and be buried in France, the glorious land of 'Liberty, Equality and Fraternity,' than to return to find America unsafe for them, though they have made the world safe for democracy."
— Charles S. Smith

Courtesy Jack Deo, Superior View

Striking miners dressed up for this picture outside the offices of the Calumet Miners' Union.

1914 *'A volcano of discontent'*

Copper Country strike is bitter and bloody

Christmas 1913 had been bitter for Michigan's Copper Country. Five months into a miners' strike, someone shouted "Fire!" at a Christmas Eve party on the second floor of a union hall. There was no fire, but the ensuing panic killed 74 people, most of them children. Gov. Woodbridge Ferris, who had sent the entire Michigan National Guard to Houghton County to keep the peace, went to the area in January to see the strike for himself. He completed his tour on Jan. 11, five days after his 61st birthday, and wrote this letter to his children.

My Dear Children:

One week ago today, I was planning my trip into the Copper Country. Today I am at home, having taken the trip. Notwithstanding my repeated announcements that I had no hope of settling the strike, the papers announce that I failed. I accomplished what I set out to accomplish.

Many of my friends did not think it safe for me to go. To be absolutely frank, there is always danger in a territory where EVERYBODY sees "RED." It would take pages; yes, a book, to tell you all about the situation. There are as usual two sides to the dispute, but as I have said one thousand times, it is a fight for the recognition of the Western Federation of Miners.

Indirectly, it is an effort on the part of socialists in the Copper Country — "red" socialists — to further their cause. I met Berger of Milwaukee, Russell of New York, Stedman of Chicago — rampant socialists.

(Socialist Party members Victor Berger, Charles Edward Russell and Seymour Stedman.) What do they care about this strike? Just enough to use the strike for socialism.

If you could only know what I know, your blood would boil. The men of wealth, in all forms, are asleep over a volcano of discontent and anarchy. An industrial, or rather an economic, revolution is fast approaching.

The socialist, anarchist, press in the Copper Country should be put out of business. It fans the flames of the basest and most brutal passions. The mine owners are not angels. Too long they have waited. Capital and labor should be twins — should co-operate.

The next day, Ferris issued a tamer statement to the press. He was "certain that if the miners had been allowed to treat with the operators as miners and not as representatives of any organization, the strike would have been settled long ago," he said. In April, with the Western Federation of Miners running out of money and divided by dissension, miners voted to end the strike. They had struck for eight-hour days, a raise to $3.50 a day and union recognition. They went back to earn $3 for an eight-hour day, but the mine owners never recognized the union and it disappeared from the Michigan copper ranges. From the Woodbridge Ferris papers in the Michigan Historical Collections at the University of Michigan's Bentley Historical Library.

Michigan Historical Collections, University of Michigan

Rebecca Shelley was a peace activist from before World War I until after the Vietnam war.

1915 *'To help bring about peace'*

Battle Creek woman tries to stop European war

War had broken out in Europe and Rebecca Shelley's fiance, a German, had been called to active duty. The Battle Creek woman, joining the effort to stop the war, went to New York City to gather comments she hoped would persuade Henry Ford to join the anti-war campaign.

Oct. 11, 1915

Dear Papa:

First I must tell you of the wonderful results of faith. I saw Mr. Ford's secretary, who gave me a challenge to get certain statements from the foreign ambassadors. Well, I left Detroit last Tuesday, arrived in New York on Wednesday and so began to try to see the German ambassador at the Ritz-Carlton Hotel. I had to encounter a lot of private secretaries, but finally was admitted to "His Excellency," who gave me a fine interview in which he said just what I wanted to say while "regretting that he could not make the statement I wanted." Of course diplomats must be very guarded, and of course he was not talking for publication. This is really a wonderful triumph and I can truly say, "It was not I who did it but the power which worketh through me."

I believe that God has laid his hand upon me and is leading me to help bring about peace. Really, the matter is very simple. All the countries realize that the war is futile and are anxious for a chance to stop without seeming beaten. But *Americans* either don't believe it, or they want to keep up the war in order to continue their profits. Now the thing for us to do is to make some influential man like Ford see that our government takes the first step in mediation. Mr. Ford's secretary said that he would believe in the plan if I got certain statements from Count (Johann-Heinrich) von Bernstorff (the German ambassador). Well, I got those statements, and now it is only a question of time till I can see Mr. Ford. I have also interviewed one Englishman of note, as well as an equally noted Englishwoman. And what they, especially the latter, told me almost makes my spirit fly out of my body. We have the blood of those people on our hands. We are the only neutral nation which is holding back from mediation. You see, it isn't enough to offer — we must call together the council of neutrals, and make definite propositions, and then the belligerents can accept without seeming to be beaten.

In the left-hand margin on the first page of her letter, Shelley wrote: "Do not tell the children of this letter. No one must know until the proper time. This is why I cannot work with moneyed organizations. This is a matter of faith, not of propaganda." Shelley was with Henry Ford aboard his Peace Ship when it set sail for Europe in December 1915, but the effort disintegrated. The United States entered the war in April 1917 and Shelley's fiance died of encephalitis before it was over. She lost her U.S. citizenship from 1922 to 1944 for marrying another German and then refusing to take a naturalization oath that required her to promise to bear arms to defend the United States. Between 1968 and 1977, she wore mourning clothes to protest the Vietnam war; she died in 1984 at age 97. From the Rebecca Shelley papers, box one, in the Michigan Historical Collections at the University of Michigan's Bentley Historical Library.

1915 *'Detroit can be cleaned out'*

Evangelist is called in to help Detroit in the fight against demon drink

Detroit's civic reformers were at fever pitch in late 1915 as they tried to rid the city of vice and liquor. Licensing fees squeezed saloon keepers, who in turn squeezed their patrons. By staying open after hours and Sundays, selling to minors and becoming hangouts for pickpockets and prostitutes, some saloons sacrificed social acceptance for profits. Local prohibition elections, which could come every other year, also put pressure on brewers and bartenders to trade beer for ballots. Angry citizens, civic figures and business leaders joined forces to regain control of the city. One was Henry Leland, president of Cadillac Motor Co. and the Detroit Citizens League. Looking for help in the next fall's statewide vote on prohibition, Leland wrote to a fist-shaking, platform-pounding, liquor-hating baseball player-turned-evangelist, the Rev. William "Billy" Sunday, on Dec. 14, 1915.

Henry Leland, the industrialist who fought alcohol.

I have noted with very deep regret the possibility that you might not plan to come to Detroit, as it had originally been hoped you would do. Those of us who have lived here many years are proud of our city and believe that industrially, and in many other respects, it is the foremost city on the continent today. We recognize, however, that it is so easy for people to become self-satisfied with their religion and their politics when they are prosperous that it is necessary for a prophet of God, such as I firmly believe you are, to give them a keener sense of their religious and civic duties. I am convinced that the time is ripe in our city for a great revival under your leadership.

My point of view is that of the city itself. Citizens have organized and battled against organized corruption. Our last two city elections have been thorough defeats of the machine gangs which breed and protect our civic and social rottenness. They are now on

the defensive, but we lack sufficient strength to rout them. A strong ally at this time would put Detroit clean and make it not only the busiest but the cleanest city, because the decent young men who are now climbing into the saddle have courage and vision.

This is really the beginning of a new era for Detroit. We are growing so fast that betterment agencies, including the churches, cannot line up people as fast as they come and the fear is that organized righteousness will lose these people and that the future life of the city will be determined poorly unless a movement large enough to attract and arrest the whole city brings them out *now*.

This invitation affords you the huge opportunity of training up a city in the way it should go. Detroit is starting all over again. It is now in the formative period; optimism and enthusiasm reign — new ideals and leaders are coming to the front. We know that what the larger Detroit of the future will be depends upon what happens now and for that reason we must have a more moral city than any large city ever yet had. The very best is imperative when a large city is in the

Free Press files

Billy Sunday, the ballplayer who became an evangelist.

making. Detroit can be cleaned out and made white *now* — perhaps not at some later date, and to get such a city started right is worth any man's best. This is *the* opportune time for Detroit.

Further, no state will have a more desperate prohibition contest than will Michigan next year. The lines are now being drawn and feeling is already warming up. Outside of Detroit, the state is largely dry, but Detroit will next fall determine whether or not the whole state shall be wet or dry. Whether we are ready for it or not, the fact is that the forces will be lined up against each other; decency against corruption, and in such a contest and at such a critical time, decency must prevail.

Billy Sunday came to save Detroit the next September. He held an 11-week revival in a tent at Woodward and Forest, preaching as many as three times a day and four times on Sundays. Newspapers reported that more than one million people — more than the city's population — came to hear him. But Detroit voters turned thumbs down on prohibition in November. People in the rest of the state, however, gave it enough votes to pass. Nationwide prohibition was enacted in 1919. From the Detroit Citizens League's correspondence files, box three, at the Burton Historical Collection, Detroit Public Library.

133

1916 'The State of Superior'

Upper Peninsula publisher says it can stand alone

Roger Andrews and his mission were well known throughout the Upper Peninsula, or Clover-Land, as he sometimes called it. When he took the floor at the banquet of the Calumet Businessmen's Association on Jan. 6, 1916, there was little doubt what the editor and publisher from Menominee wanted to talk about: UP independence.

The Upper Peninsula comprises nearly one-third of all the area of the great State of Michigan, the largest state, excepting Georgia, east of the Mississippi River.

The Upper Peninsula at no place touches the Lower Peninsula, but the former is bounded by its thousand miles of lake shore, touching three of the five Great Lakes, and 180 miles of borderline adjoining the State of Wisconsin.

The Upper Peninsula is larger than Delaware, Massachusetts and Connecticut combined.

The Upper Peninsula has a larger population than Delaware, Idaho, Wyoming, Arizona, Nevada or New Mexico.

Situated in the upper half of the north temperate zone, the Upper Peninsula of Michigan has sunshine more than 12 hours every day from March 20th to Sept. 22 and, in June, the sun shines about 16 hours out of the 24. This means successful farming, for the soil is fertile and its development has only been delayed because of the large operation in lumbering and mining which, great as they are and have been, are now to be followed by the turning into profitable farms of some seven million acres.

There is no reason under the broad canopy of heaven why this great empire of the Upper Peninsula, rich in every natural gift, endowed by nature beyond so many of these United States, a garden spot of agricultural opportunity, a center of

From Clover-Land Magazine

The magazine cover is from the first issue of Andrews' magazine, Clover-Land.

industrial and commercial activity, the home of a third of a million people, industrious, thrifty and patriotic, should not now take its rightful place among the states of the Union.

There is room in Old Glory for another star.

And that star, "The State of Superior."

The speech was published on the front page of the Jan. 6, 1916, Menominee Herald-Leader and reprinted in James L. Carter's "Superior: A State for the North Country," the Pilot Press, Marquette, 1980: page 39.

Free Press files

Detroiters wave flags before a replica of the Statue of Liberty — used in World War I bond drives — on Armistice Day, Nov. 11, 1918.

1918 *'Behind the men behind the guns'*

Students join the war effort with pennies, clean plates

The United States was totally involved in World War I by 1918 — on both sides of the Atlantic. American men were dying over there, and people over here were doing what they could to help the war effort. Students throughout Michigan entered an essay contest, writing about the war effort in their schools and communities. The first excerpts are from an essay by Donald Ross of Ypsilanti, winner in the over-15 category.

It is now nearly two years since the American nation entered into the war across the sea. When our declaration of war came, nations had been using men as targets for three years. Germany had been stopped, but still she was pressing hard on the human border of France. Things looked dubious for the Allies. Everyone was well acquainted with the way of the Hun, his way of crucifying innocent non-combatants. It was then that the United States came to life and went over the top to save the day.

However, the boys in khaki were not the only stars that played in the hero parts in the largest and grimmest tragedy of all history. Most of us know what has been done by our boys overseas, but to some it is vague what has taken place back behind the men behind the guns. The purpose of this writing is to show just what has taken place here, especially in Ypsilanti.

Our streets were bare of autos for many Sundays; the Ypsilanti motorists were heeding the call of their country. They were more than willing to give up what gasoline they would use in their Sunday pleasure riding if it could be of any value in the winning of the war. It was a glorious thought that filled the minds of many sitting at home, thinking that the gasoline which they had saved that day was speeding a tank over "no man's land," dealing its missiles of death to the Hun and bringing disorder and retreat to his lines.

The ragmen were for once cheated out of their supplies by the city's patriotism. We had read in our papers of the way in which the Hun was ravaging northern France and Belgium and how he was driving the poor inhabitants out, homeless, penniless. Such stories were sufficient to touch the hardest heart. As the call for clothes for the needy "over there" came, the townspeople rushed to the appointed place with their last year's garments. All told, nearly 5,000 pounds of clothes was the glorious result.

Alma Gilbert, winner in the under-15 category, wrote this about the war effort in

Saginaw:

Each night a group of boys and girls stayed after school to work. Most of the girls wore aprons and Red Cross caps to make themselves feel more like real Red Cross workers. Every week we had tape to cut in 10-inch strips, then these were placed in piles of sixes and put in small envelopes. Usually there were from 500 to 1,000 of these envelopes to fill. We also had buttons to count out and put sometimes seven, and sometimes eight, buttons in an envelope. This work saved the ladies hours of their valuable time (making clothing).

Different things were made in the separate rooms, some of them very important to help the poor little children of Belgium. A couple of the rooms collected woolen blocks from the tailors, sewed them together, padded, lined and tied them, making quilts for the Belgian babies.

The boys of the seventh and eighth grades had been saving money for quite a while to buy baseball suits. When they saw so much money was needed they rose to the occasion and turned the money over to the Red Cross. Oh, yes, it was rather hard, but they saw that our government needed the money more than they needed baseball suits. Even the little first graders did their share in this. They licked their plates clean for Mr. Hoover and took some of their playtime to help their mothers and run errands.

Herbert Hoover was director of the U.S. Committee for Relief in Belgium from 1915 to 1919. He was elected president in 1929. From Bulletin No. 11 of the Michigan Historical Commission, Lansing, 1919: pages 6-9 and 14-17.

1918 'A great big circus'

Detroiter tours Europe with pack on his back

It had been almost 18 months since President Woodrow Wilson, spurred by the sinking of five American ships, asked Congress for a declaration of war on Germany. At the time, April 1917, some said the United States would end the 32-month-old war before Christmas. It was not to be. In the fall of 1918, Pvt. Leo Beslock of Detroit was marching across Europe with the 310th Engineers. His letters home gave a foot soldier's view of Europe.

Sept. 17

Left the small town we were in and are at present repairing roads. Been doing a lot of hiking from town to town and am seeing a lot of France. Most of the towns are all demolished and some have no inhabitants. Have been in a couple of air raids but there is not much danger.

See lots of Americans around and they are a hard-boiled bunch. Woodward Avenue has nothing on the traffic down some of these roads. It reminds a fellow of a great big circus.

Prices are very high here and a fellow begins to dislike the storekeepers. A hat full of grapes are 90 cents and a small can of sardines or salmon is 75 cents. I am fairly well flushed with the wallpaper they call money so don't mind too much.

Oct. 16

Been camped in tents for about a week now. Dig a hole in the ground big enough for two or three men. The hole is about three feet deep; bank the sides with bags full of earth, stretch the tent over it. Generally put boards or tin on the bottom, get some straw, hay or bags on them, overcoats and two blankets next. Then we have three blankets and raincoats to cover up with. We have supper about six p.m. and by this time it is

Courtesy Caroline Smith Beslock

Leo Beslock in uniform

137

dark. Smoke a pipe and in bed by 7 p.m.

Most of the time, the roar of the guns do not let you fall asleep. We used to have frequent gas alarms at night but I have never been through gas so far.

I saw a woman for the first time in a month the other day.

On Nov. 11, 1918, the Allies and Germany signed the Armistice, ending the war. Although the shooting had stopped, the marching went on.

Dec. 1

I see in the Stars and Stripes, an English paper, that the boys are anxious to go into Germany. I have found that is not the case in our outfit and I know it is not the case here with me. If it is the fastest way home, it would be great. As for seeing the country with a full pack on your back, it is no joke. After we hit a burg we do not have any time to see it anyway. We are in St. Mard, (Belgium) but cannot go to Virton, which is about like being in Windsor and not being able to visit Detroit.

Dec. 17

Two of the fellows received their Xmas boxes yesterday and we have a paper Xmas tree on the table now. I wish I had wrote for cigars, as I can get all the sweets I want now. But two months ago a box of chocolate looked like the world to me.

I see they have changed some of the (troop) transports into liners already and that they are full coming here. I would like to see them hold all the second-hand excitement seekers for about six months at least. There is nothing here to see.

After the war, Beslock returned to Detroit, where he was a finish carpenter and made jewelry. He lived in the family home on Roosevelt with his wife and stepson and died in 1963. From letters donated by Leo Beslock's niece, Caroline Smith Beslock, to the Michigan Historical Collections at the University of Michigan's Bentley Historical Library.

1919 *'Freedom must be their reward'*

Black soldiers want to share the rights they defended

Less than three months after the Armistice was signed in Europe, Bishop Charles S. Smith of the African Methodist Episcopal Church in Detroit was worried about how returning black soldiers would be received. Bishop Smith, a former member of the Alabama House of Representatives, wrote of his concerns in a Feb. 8, 1919, letter to the National Negro Press Association, meeting in Nashville.

Michigan Historical Collections, University of Michigan

Charles S. Smith Sr.   Charles S. Smith Jr.

In my opinion, leaders of various Negro groups are displaying a woeful lack of mental perception and vision. For instance, they are frothing over great international questions, such as the disposition which should be made of the German colonies in Africa, the interests of native African races, etc., while they are quiescent on subjects of paramount interest to our boys overseas. There are problems at home of more vital importance to them than any which are centered in Europe.

The treatment that is accorded our boys on their return from the blood-stained battlefields of France, especially those whose homes are beneath southern skies, should be our first consideration. On this subject, I regret to note that, with few exceptions, the Negro press has been ominously silent.

The spirit of our boys overseas is reflected in the following statements, which I quote from a personal letter received from one of them:

"I want you to know that our boys are giving a good account of themselves. They are making the supreme sacrifice willingly and nobly. They are fighting shoulder to shoulder with seasoned troops and are reaching every objective outlined for them. Indeed, this is a great education for our young men, many of whom have never been outside the limits of their own small

localities. They, too, are tasting freedom and will come back a strong, virile force, demanding those inalienable rights so long denied them. And this time they will be worthy. They will have fought for freedom and freedom must be their reward."

With this spirit obsessing the Negro combatants now overseas and with the revival of the Ku Klux Klan in Georgia and Tennessee for the purposes of keeping the demobilized Negro troops "in their places" on their return to their homes, it seems to me that the time is opportune for the Negro press to agitate the convening of an inter-racial conference of southern leaders to try and reach an agreement on the best course to pursue to avoid race friction and to insure the dominance of peace and order.

Far better that our sons should die and be buried in France, the glorious land of "Liberty, Equality and Fraternity," than to return to find America unsafe for them, though they have made the world safe for democracy.

Bishop Smith had more than one meaning when he wrote about "our sons" fighting for freedom in France. His son, Charles S. Smith Jr., was a lieutenant in the war. From the Charles Spencer Smith papers, box one, in the Michigan Historical Collections at the University of Michigan's Bentley Historical Library.

1920 '500 Negroes on this train'

Booming automobile factories bring in black workers

Black workers from the South arrived daily in Detroit during 1920 to satisfy a demand for labor created by World War I. Between 1910 and 1920, Michigan's black population more than tripled, rising from 17,115 to 60,082. By 1930, it was more than 169,000, as more and more workers found jobs in Michigan's expanding post-war economy. Forrester B. Washington, executive director of the Detroit Urban League from 1916 to 1918, reported on the trend in his position as research director for Associated Charities of Detroit.

The great war has worked a miracle in the industrial status of the Negro in Detroit. The extent to which Negroes have gone into employment in the manufacturing concerns in the city is astounding to one who bears in mind the situation 10 years ago, or even five years ago.

We find, as a result of our survey, that there are 15,000 Negroes employed in the business establishments of this city. This means that there are three times as many Negroes working in the automobile plants, the foundries and the merchandise establishments of the city as there were Negroes living in the city at the census of 1910.

In what is Detroit's chief industry, namely, the manufacture of automobiles, there were only 183 Negroes engaged in the whole country in 1910. Today there are 8,000 Negroes engaged in the automobile industry in Detroit alone.

The most surprising feature of the investigation into the industrial status of the Negro in Detroit is the variety of occupations into which he has entered during the past five years. The narrow limits of porter, elevator-operator and waiter within which the Negro was practically confined up until 1915 have been extended to include car maker, engineer, millwright, moulder, toolmaker, riveter, dairy worker, chipper, grinder, welder, punch-press operator, heat treater, galvanizer, chassis and frame assembler, crane operator, timekeeper, cigar stripper, paint mixer, varnish cooker and so on to 179 different occupations.

Not nearly as many Negroes were brought to Detroit by labor agents (recruiters) as were brought by labor agents to other cities. Where labor agents did not work out of Detroit, they were sent by two foundries and one automobile concern.

Many authorities are inclined to believe that the Negro migration has decreased. There is no basis for this belief.

As a matter of fact, one day during the past summer the largest number of Negroes that ever came to Detroit on one train arrived from Birmingham, Ala. There were over 500 Negroes on this train. Most of them were farm laborers, which was an unusual departure because most of the groups arriving are about evenly divided between rural and urban Negroes. There must have been some stimulation to this particular group. It may have been the result of an indirect recruiting conducted in the South by colored men for one or more Detroit plants. There are good reasons for believing that this sort of thing is done occasionally in Detroit even today.

The Associated Charities of Detroit was forerunner of the United Foundation. Forrester B. Washington lived until 1963, when he died at age 74. From Washington's 1920 report, "The Negro in Detroit: A Survey of the Conditions of a Negro Group in a Northern Industrial Center During the War Prosperity Period:" pages 2-11.

Archives of Labor and Urban Affairs, Wayne State University

Many Detroit factories used black workers in their foundries.

1921 *'Fish that weigh 60 pounds'*

Big fish, open spaces in northern Michigan

John Fritz had fished many lakes, but few teemed with life as Houghton Lake did in August 1921. In letters home to Columbus, Ohio, he told his wife, Emma, and daughters Hellen and Ruth about fishing on Michigan's largest inland lake.

We had a great trip. We made the trip in 23 hours. The last 30 miles to the lake, we had to follow an old Indian trail through the bushes and woods. It was just wide enough for the auto to go through and the sand was hub deep, so we had to go very slow.

This is a wonderful place. I was out fishing this morning a little while. I caught one that was just as long as my arm and five not quite so large, and one I suppose would have weighed 40 pounds got away. I did not have any reel or I would have landed it. There were about 100 caught right near me.

The weather is fine up here. There are lots of porcupines up here and lots of bear and deer. It is a very large lake, 14 miles one way and much larger the other way. They catch fish that weigh 60 pounds. We have a new cottage for $14 a week. There are hundreds of thousands of acres of sand, mostly woods, that nobody lives on.

We catch so many that we don't know what to do with them. Every new load (of people) that comes in here, we give them a load of fish. We go out behind a tugboat. There are 10 or 12 rowboats tied on behind it. We go out five or six miles. We catch all kinds of fish. Lots of big pike. Some are so large that we cannot land them. I have caught 12 as large as my arm and larger, and bushels of smaller ones.

The bottom is sand. You can wade out a mile. Most things are just as cheap up here as they are at home.

We have to fish with wire lines. The fish bite the others off and get away, and sometimes they bite the wire. Some of the

From a postcard by Etha Smith

The caption on one of the postcards Fritz mailed home said "Fair enough for one afternoon — Houghton Lake."

big ones take you on a merry ride with a big anchor that you can hardly lift. Folks fish off the big tugboat that pulls us out. It stays out until we come in.

They are having some big forest fires north of here but no danger here. It cannot get to us for the lake. We passed 20 lakes on the road up here. There are people here from all over the United States.

We took a ride up to Indian River through the wilderness. The forest fires ran over thousands of acres. Our cottage is on a hill and we look out over the lake. You can't fish off the bank as it is too shallow. Sometimes the tugboat has a string of boats tied on behind as long as from home to High Street. It looks funny to see them going out.

With lots of love from Daddy.

Fritz owned a lake development in Ohio in the early 1900s and died in 1959. His letters were submitted by his niece, Eileen Rankin of Mt. Pleasant, who recalls weeks and weekends at his cottage on Indian Lake in Ohio.

Hard times

"We're so poor now and my brother Eddie needs books for high school and we can't buy (them) for we have no money and I want him to study for he has set his mind to be a druggist. He's more important than I am."

— Stella Ladoska

1926 *'Shots of their guns in the night'*

Raid helps turn industrialist against Prohibition

Calvin Coolidge was in the White House in 1926, "Bye Bye Blackbird" was a top tune and bootleggers were in their heyday. Up and down the Detroit River, rum-running had become a running battle. Henry B. Joy, founder and president of Packard Motor Car Co., wrote to Prohibition enforcement officials on Dec. 19 to complain about a raid on his St. Clair Shores property.

During the summer months, when my boat house and harbor have been accessible by boats which have brought alcoholic beverages and landed them there, I have raised no objection to the visits of the federal officers. I have heard the shots of their guns in the night; the whole situation has been very annoying, but I could see no way of curing the difficulties. I certainly had no way of stopping the incoming boats and the United States government was unable to stop the boats, in spite of the shootings, etc.

I did feel, however, that in wintertime, with the premises ice-locked and no boats having access, that I would be free from the invasion of the Prohibition officers. However, that has not proved the case.

The facts of this raid upon my premises, so far as I can ascertain them, are that two men in civilian clothes came to my boat house about 6 o'clock (Dec. 9) and asked admission from my watchman and he naturally let them in. They began to rummage about and search the premises and my watchman sent his son to a nearby police station for an officer to help him put them out.

When the police officer arrived, they informed him that they were federal Prohibition officers and that they had orders from the downtown headquarters office to search Joy's boat house. They searched in every corner, opening all lockers, breaking open some, and found, as I am informed, 11 bottles of beer, which my aged watchman, Frank Gifford, had there.

I could not see what good purpose was served by molesting my watchman; no supply of liquor was found which could, by any stretch of the imagination, indicate that the premises were being used to store liquor for traffic and trade purposes.

I have heard and read of rude searchings and shootings, sometimes fatal, by Prohibition officers, but I never before have come personally in contact with the carrying on by the United States government of this civil war, as I call it, in which about one-half of the people are arrayed against the other half of the people.

I want to express my appreciation of the courtesy of your people in refraining from destroying bottles captured on my premises, and (not) throwing the refuse glass into the waters where in summertime the children and grown-ups go swimming.

Joy had originally supported Prohibition, but later worked to end it, calling his earlier position "stupidly wrong." From the Henry Bourne Joy papers, box one, in the Michigan Historical Collections at the University of Michigan's Bentley Historical Library.

Free Press photo

Henry B. Joy in 1933, after he had come to regret his "stupidly wrong" support of Prohibition.

1930 'Wettest town in the country'

Rumrunning turns the coast into a battleground

Detroit's reputation for rum-running received so much attention in the late '20s that the "Detroit-Windsor funnel" was perhaps as well known as the soon to be completed Detroit-Windsor Tunnel. An article in the March 1930 issue of Plain Talk magazine contributed to that reputation under the headline "Michigan — Soused and Serene."

Detroit today is the wettest and widest open town in the country and has the largest per capita consumption of liquor of all the cities in the United States — New York included.

The federal government maintains a small army and navy in the Detroit sector in the effort to check smuggling from Canada. There are two 75-foot Coast Guard cutters stationed at Detroit, one 36-foot patrol boat and about 30 speedboats in the dry flotilla, and the fleet is manned by some 30 Coast Guardsmen.

The dry army consists of 150 customs officials; 50 members of the Immigration Service border patrol; some 30 federal Prohibition agents, and about 10 members of the narcotic squad. Despite frequent killings — 44 persons have been slain by federal dry agents in Michigan — the profits are so alluring that liquor keeps flowing across the Detroit River all along the 102-mile front from Ecorse to Port Huron, in winter as well as summer.

When the river freezes, the rumrunners cross the ice, towing toboggans behind automobiles or having men on skates push sleds. When the river is open, liquor is brought across in small outboard speedboats. Many of the speedboats have ice runners on their bottoms. From Ecorse to the River Rouge, the entire American shore of the Detroit River is lined almost solidly

Free Press photo

Two bottles were saved for evidence from this 1931 seizure of four speedboats and 196 cases of beer. The rest of the beer went into the Detroit River.

with boat houses, houseboats, and houses built down to the river containing "boat wells." Off Ecorse the river is dotted with islands, and opposite the city of Detroit the rumrunners can take shelter behind Belle Isle.

The rumrunners can dash from the Canadian waters to the American shore in two minutes in speedboats and they have an elaborate system of signals by their "airedales," which usually permits the "monkeys" to land the cargoes unmolested. "Gorillas" guard the landing operations. The boats crossed the river in two minutes and 40 seconds and the cases of liquor were unloaded into waiting autos in less than 50 seconds. Then "gorillas" held back traffic on side streets while the autos sped away.

In many respects Detroit is the most modern city in America — and the most American. It has had a more rapid growth

Free Press photo

Prohibition officers break up or "knock off" a still during the early '30s.

than any large American city, and its development, which started and kept pace with the automobile industry, almost seems to epitomize the progress of our modern age — and the era of mass production.

Unfortunately, Detroit is located in Michigan and Michigan is one of the states where 60 percent of the people who reside in cities are governed by the 40 percent who live on the farms. The upcountry legislators who followed the Anti-Saloon League and Ku Klux Klan attempted to impose their pre-war rural morality on this great modern Babylon, with the result that harmless habits were outlawed; the law was made a thing to spit upon, graft inevitably grew; and

today the gangsters and crooked politicians have formed an alliance that is slowly but surely paralyzing all branches of the government.

In February 1933, Congress proposed a constitutional amendment repealing Prohibition. Michigan became the first state to vote for Prohibition's repeal on April 3. By the end of the year, the amendment had been ratified by 36 states and was approved. From Walter W. Liggett, "Michigan, Soused and Serene," the March 1930 issue of Plain Talk, copyright 1930, New York: pages 257-273.

147

1931 *'There are many unemployed'*

A child of the Great Depression adopts the mayor as her uncle

During the Great Depression, hundreds of people wrote to Detroit Mayor Frank Murphy to ask for jobs, money and favors. One girl in her mid-teens, Stella Ladoska, asked for something different. She wanted to adopt him as her uncle.

June 7

Dear Sir,

I am dropping a few lines to tell you, or ask you again, to let me see the City Hall and police station. I have time from June 18th till Sept. for it's vacation then and in Sept. I have to go to high school in Flint for the deaf.

I would like to become a "police girl" for a few days or weeks during my vacation. I hope you won't refuse this, for if you don't want, you don't need to do it for you are a mayor. This is the first and last wish I ever asked a mayor.

I guess you can let a deaf girl be a police girl if you want to for a few weeks or days. I could work Sundays at Cecil and McGraw or Martin between Parkwood and Waldo. During days I could walk around and see if everything goes right. I don't want any wages for that's to help the city. So I won't take any. I guess our city (needs) money now anyway. There are many unemployed.

Stella toured police headquarters on June 24.

Aug. 3

Dear Mr. Murphy,

I am thanking you for your kindness to me. You have let me have a few minutes and permitted me to shake hands with you, and let me see City Hall and police headquarters, which I always wanted to see.

Your term is expiring soon and I wish you will win again to be a mayor of Detroit, for you have done good. Even though I am small, I can see the works you have made were good to the poor people who needed the help of an executive to rule them. I hope that you will let me write to you from Flint as a friend even if you won't be a mayor.

In my other letters to you, I will call you "Uncle Frankie." I have no uncles, so I want you to be mine, for a girlfriend of mine has so many aunts and uncles. That's why I want to have at least you as an uncle. And when you write to me to Flint, you must write "Your Loving Uncle" so I could show her that I have an uncle. Is that fair?

Sept.

Dear Uncle Frankie,

I have here (in Flint) the most unhappy time. All the girls say I must study signs and some of the teachers say (so) too. But I don't want to. Oh, how lonesome I am for my mother. I do wish I could go to Detroit High School. The girls over here don't want to talk to me for I don't know sign.

Sept. 30.

Dear Uncle Frankie,

I am writing this letter in happiness. I am back home and walking to school over here for the hearing children and for lip reading to my old school.

The teachers in Flint talk sign and if I would of studied sign I would of forgot how to talk. Besides, mother isn't well. Kidney trouble.

I wonder when will Ford start working. Dad isn't working since I last saw you and we must pay for the house, gas, electric, water and tax bills, of course grocery, and we don't know from where we shall get the money. Dad and mommy are worrying and it's bad for mother. I hope I can help them, but no one would take me to work so I'm asking you to get me a job after school. Could you, Uncle Frank?

We're so poor now and my brother Eddie

Free Press files

Many people wrote to Detroit Mayor Frank Murphy in the early '30s, but few adopted him as an uncle.

needs books for high school and we can't buy (them) for we have no money and I want him to study for he has set his mind to be a druggist. He's more important than I am.

Nov. 14

Dear Uncle Frankie,

I'm just dropping a few lines as usual. Gee, I do congratulate you for fighting so hard, and you sure won. Sometimes when I write I dream that I'm talking to you and not writing. And I'm pouring everything that comes to my mind. I guess it's very impolite to write in pencil to a mayor. But you see that my writing even in pencil is not so good. What about ink?

Dad still isn't working, but men around my house are beginning to work. I hope that dad shall go before Christmas, don't you? We shall have a pretty unhappy Christmas it seems, and so will many other people.

From the Mayor's Papers for 1931, box six, Burton Historical Collection, Detroit Public Library.

1932 *'Not of bullets, but of ballots'*

The radio priest of Royal Oak ignites the nation's passions

"Golden Hour of the Little Flower" was a Sunday tradition for as many as 30 million Americans in the 1930s. They tuned in to hear the Rev. Charles Coughlin, the radio priest of Royal Oak, comment on society, politics, business and religion. Father Coughlin named the show for the Shrine of the Little Flower he had been commissioned to build at Woodward Avenue and Twelve Mile Road. On March 13, 1932, Father Coughlin took up poverty, labor unrest and communism.

Yesterday afternoon, a vast throng of Detroiters gathered to attend the simple funeral of four slain men. It was simple in one sense. In another, it was unique to see a procession of 10,000 marching men, not one of them carrying an American flag. There were plenty of red flags.

As you know, last week there was a demonstration in which some of Detroit's jobless, suffering laborers participated. We since learned that this demonstration had been organized by the communists. However, the thousands of those who marched through the streets of the city of Detroit were orderly and were obedient in every respect to the policemen who accompanied them. By no means were they all communists.

The object of the demonstrators was to march to the Ford automobile factories which are located not in Detroit, but in the city of Dearborn adjacent to Detroit.

It appears that the jobless marchers had determined to send a delegation from their ranks to the Ford executives to ask for part-time jobs. But when they approached the Ford factory, radical leaders urged them to trespass upon private property. Promptly they were halted; greeted with tear gas bombs; covered with ice-cold water, which was shot at them out of a fire hose, and eventually bombarded with bullets as they persisted in their trespassing.

Now, what has been foreshadowed at the Ford factory in Dearborn, Mich., is but the beginning of a tragedy that will be enacted on the streets of America if we permit the radicals to assume the leadership of our discontented and jobless citizenry.

If a shot fired at Lexington or Concord was heard round the world, so the shots fired at Dearborn shall not be easily muffled unless we bend every effort not only to relieve the laborer from his distressing conditions but also to lead him thoughtfully and surely away from the siren voice of destructive communism.

Laboring men, I have a word for you: Place no undue blame upon the shoulders of Henry Ford. Undoubtedly he has done his best during this year of Depression to supply work and food and shelter to many thousands.

My friend the laborer, I have been most outspoken in coming to your defense. Will you hear me and believe me when I tell you of the communism which is dicing for your approval and for your support?

They want revolution by blood, by slaughter. And you want peace and work and happiness gained through the power, not of bullets, but of ballots.

Mr. Laboring Man, no one with intelligence wants to become a communist. Communism is nothing more than an unintelligent effort to escape from the idleness and the poverty; from the political favoritism; from the unjust concentration of wealth in the hands of a few, and from the unsupportable taxation which threaten us.

Be intelligent and use the American method of ballots — not the Bolshevik method of bullets.

Wide World Photo

Millions of people listened to the Rev. Charles Coughlin's radio sermons regularly in the 1930 and '40s.

Father Coughlin's radio show, which had begun gently in 1926, became increasingly political and popular throughout the 1930s. In 1934, postal officials said no one in the country was getting more mail than Coughlin. By 1940, traces of anti-Semitism and pro-Hitlerism had crept into his speeches and in 1942, Cardinal Edward Mooney, archbishop of Detroit, silenced Father Coughlin on direct orders from Pope Pius XII. Father Coughlin died in 1979 at age 88. From "Father Coughlin's Radio Discourses, 1931-1932," the Radio League of the Little Flower, Royal Oak, March 1932: pages 227-239.

1934 *'I am learning the ropes'*

CCC gives thousands of men jobs, money and hope

Frank Munger, 18, earned $30 a month at Civilian Conservation Corps camps near Rapid River in 1933 and near Munising in 1934. He had agreed to have $25 sent home each month, so he supplemented the $5 he kept by cutting hair at 10 cents a head. The wages were meager, but in the midst of the Great Depression and widespread unemployment, CCC provided a measure of security for thousands. These excerpts are from Munger's 1934 diary.

Jan. 2

We arrived at camp at 11:30 from Grand Rapids. We ate dinner and rested the rest of the afternoon.

Jan. 6

I worked the forenoon in the root cellar. This afternoon I cut hair.

Jan. 7

It was a warm day. I was on K.P. all day. One of the trucks hauling wood tipped over and hurt one of the fellows bad.

Jan. 15

Five of us went about 10 miles to get poles for the root cellar roof. We had snowshoes to walk on. It was the first time I've used them.

Feb. 1

Today was payday. I had $3.55 left from my wages.

Feb. 4

The snow is pretty deep now. We played stud poker nearly all day. I was about 70 cents ahead.

Feb. 9

It was about 35 below zero this morning. Today is the last day I work on the root cellar.

Feb. 13

Today was the first day that I worked in the woods, cutting and burning brush in five feet of snow.

Feb. 25

We ate out of plates for the first time today. (The men had been using mess kits.) We had chicken and pie.

March 3

I went to the dentist's and had a tooth pulled and one filled. (This was Munger's first visit to a dentist.) It cost three dollars. I bought eight pounds of raisins for 62 cents.

March 8

The captain asked me to take the dispensary job at First Aid station.

March 10

I am learning the ropes pretty fast in first aid. We are treating about seven fellows for lacerations of the feet and hands.

March 27

It was a nice day. I cut the captain's and the lieutenant's hair today. They each gave me 20 cents.

April 22

We had chicken for dinner. I pounded a typewriter for the first time today. It snowed a little today.

May 6

I earned $1 this afternoon cutting hair. Some of the fellows were called out to fight fires already.

May 12

We cleaned up the barracks this morning. I and another fellow went to Marquette to a show. I bought $8 worth of clothes.

June 1

They had a dance at Camp Wyman in the

Courtesy Frank Munger

CCC workers eat lunch in July, 1933, during a break from fighting fires near Rapid River.

day room. There were a lot of girls from Munising there. We had punch and cake and doughnuts for refreshments.

June 10

We fellows who have been in the CCC a year had our annual picnic in the old campgrounds at Rapid River. We had 32 gallons of beer and lots of girls.

June 22

We worked in the woods. The mosquitoes were pretty thick but I had some dope that kept them away.

July 10

Today is the day we leave the CCC. I have spent exactly 13 months and 22 days in the outfit.

The CCC was established in 1933 and disbanded in 1942. During those years, 100,000 men, most aged 17 to 28, worked in Michigan's approximately 120 camps. This diary was submitted by Munger, who went on to a career in the Navy and later became a real estate salesman in Grand Rapids.

Courtesy Lyn Powrie Davidge

Emerson F. Powrie and
Gwendolyn Sutton at his
graduation from the University
of Michigan in June, 1936.

1934 *'I'll be cutting paper dolls'*

College student suffers through red tape, job hunt

After an interruption for the Great Depression, Emerson F. Powrie had returned to school as a junior at the University of Michigan. During his two years there, he and sweetheart Gwendolyn Sutton exchanged about 200 letters. She was a teacher at the Michigan School for the Deaf in Flint, their hometown.

Sept. 18

Dear Gwen:

Before I came down here I used to think that the Buick Motor Car Co. was bound up with a lot of red tape when it came to getting into the place, but the Buick has to take a back seat after registering in the University of Michigan. The worst of it is that I've just started and I think by the time I'm finished I'll be cutting paper dolls or something.

Yesterday afternoon we started making the weary rounds of restaurants, but were unable to land a job.

Talk about luck, since I wrote the preceding paragraph I've been out and obtained a temporary job. The telephone rang and it was Mrs. Smith from Cutting's Cafe and she asked me to come over and see her. I hotfooted right over there and she hired me temporarily.

Sept 19

Dear Gwen:

After I arrived (at Cutting's) last night, the two regular waiters showed up and I wondered just where I stood. However, the customers came so thick and fast that we ran out of food after we had served about two-thirds of them and they also hired two new waiters on account of the rush. Also today they put on two more new men, so I really might be called an old timer, having worked four meals already.

Sept. 21

Dear Emerson:

I hadn't intended writing so soon but since you would like to receive some mail, I'll give you a little gossip besides the card although I know it isn't according to Emily Post.

(Your mother) told me that they planned to come down and see you before long and asked me to join them. Now wasn't that sweet of her? But really I haven't any interest in Ann Arbor.

I'll send you some paper dolls if you find you really need them — but if you can get along without them, why, you'll have more time for study.

Sept. 23

Dear Gwen:

Tomorrow the long, hard grind begins and who can tell where that is going to end? Down here though when I tell anyone that I'm going to study education, they shrug their shoulders and laugh, saying, "Pipe course." So perhaps the grind isn't going to be as hard as I think.

We all went down to the Michigan (Theater) and saw "Elmer and Elsie," starring George Bancroft. The show was very good, especially because they had vaudeville, but the thing that I liked best was the organ. To my mind an organ adds a lot to a show. Another thing they did was to flash words of popular songs on the screen and then while the organ played everybody joined in and sang and down here they really sing them.

Emerson graduated in 1936 and moved to Flint to teach and be near Gwen. They were married in 1937 and moved to Ann Arbor in 1945 where they taught. He became a principal and, later, a deputy superintendent of schools. Their daughter, Lyn Powrie Davidge of Ann Arbor, submitted the letters.

1937 *'The cash register plays a tune'*

Shopping carts and free coffee put Meijer on its feet

Dutch immigrant Hendrik Meijer was trying to establish a grocery business in Greenville when he described the triumphs and troubles of the late '30s in letters to his daughter, Johanna, a student at the University of Michigan.

Nov. 23, 1936

This is a cold morning and I am in the back room. Ma is in front writing welfare orders so we can get the money the first of the month. Everything is OK so far. The butcher is doing a nice business and so are we. Conditions are much improved all over the country and everything points up. I heard a radio talk that said we would even surpass 1929. If we do, we are on the ground floor.

Nov. 25, 1937

Brother and I went to Grand Rapids this week and $300 put us in the clear. I'm glad that someday we'll be able to lift the mortgage and show the bank that we don't have to kiss their feet. Roy Rossman is trying to sell the farm and maybe his home to satisfy the bank, because the Depression is not all a thing of the past.

Brother is playing the fiddle and mother is working on welfare slips. I got bawled out for putting too much bread on one order — you know, the poor do not need so much bread. Mr. Lincoln is mad at the government for buying so many apples to give to the needy. I told him that every apple bought by the government would go to people having no buying power and would help his market, because it would take care of the surplus. But he saw red and he is too good a Christian to be mistaken. You know, religion and Republicanism give

them that self-satisfying, never-to-be-wrong feeling. Some people could not see a changing world if they were dropped off on Mars.

Nov. 7, 1938

Last week Saturday we had the best day ever. We sold $982 in groceries and the meat department did $314. The new wagons (shopping carts) came in just right. At one time Brother came to me saying, "You know, all the wagons are in use," and we also have 24 baskets with handles. We bought new baskets with the wagons. They are deeper and have just small handles to lift the loads onto the counter.

Brother is going to take $1,100 to the bank this morning. — of course, that is to cover checks. That is the most we have banked at one time. Saturday was WPA payday and Gibson (Refrigerator) payday was Friday. Gibson does not mean much yet, but will soon, according to reports.

Dec. 3, 1938

Today we gave away a pound of coffee to each customer free, and they are coming from far and near, some with crutches and some in wheelchairs. You give something away and they come for it.

We have a nice ad in this week and the cash register plays a tune all the time.

Cash registers continued to play a tune for Meijer as the Thrift Market evolved into the Meijer Inc. chain of retail stores, now based in Grand Rapids. Meijer died in 1964. The letters were submitted by his grandson, also named Hendrik Meijer, who drew heavily on family letters to write "Thrifty Years," published by William B. Eerdmans Publishing Co., Grand Rapids, in 1984.

Courtesy Hendrik Meijer

In 1937, the Meijer Thrift Market advertised five pounds of sweet potatoes for 10 cents and a pound of steak for 18 cents.

Left, Meijer's Thrift Market had grown by 1940.

1937 *'Bricks, hinges, bolts flying'*

Workers stand their ground by sitting down

Years of tension at General Motors plants in Flint broke on Dec. 30, 1936, amid reports the company planned to close Fisher Body No. 1. Workers inside the plant sat down in protest and, soon, men inside other plants did the same. Some stayed until the strike ended Feb. 11. Inside Fisher Body No. 2, Francis O'Rourke kept a sitdown striker's diary.

Dec. 30, 1936

Men waving arms — they have fired some more union men. Stop the lines. Men shouting. Loud talking. The strike is on.

This strike has been coming for years. Speed-up system, seniority, overbearing foremen. You can just go so far, you know, even with working men.

Now the fellows are settling down. I never knew we had so many entertainers in this little shop. Some are dancing, others have formed a quartet — fair singers, too. Now a snake dance, everyone is asked to sing a song, do a dance or recite a poem.

Dec. 31, 1936

What will happen today? I hope it will be over. Thinking of that party at home this evening. I wonder if the basement is decorated for the occasion. There it is, 12 o'clock, whistles, cheers — 1937. Peace on Earth — why must men in the world's most perfect democracy have to take such steps to survive?

Well, the wife and all my guests are out on the street celebrating. It's sure swell, but a lump climbs into a guy's throat.

Jan. 1, 1937

Wish I had a morning paper; maybe an agreement has been made. The boys have settled down, not so much noise at night now. Did you notice the expressions on the faces? Drawn, pale, tired and anxious. Do hope this can't last much longer, for all of us are here to stay.

Jan. 11, 1937

Well, I see the heat has been shut off again, and it's getting quite cold in here. Well, let's wrap up a little warmer; we'll have no trouble about that. 6:15 p.m. Here they come! — 22 factory police with their long nightsticks. Going to take the ladders, are you? Go ahead, but why carry the clubs? What!! They have locked the doors and won't allow our dinner brought in. Why?? Those hot meals those ladies have out there will be cold in a few minutes . . . You can be cold, you know, but cold and hungry is too much. We'll push the doors open; there they go. The doors are open to us for the first time since this thing has started. Men are shaking hands with their brothers on the outside. Everyone is laughing. Let's sing a song. "Hail, Hail, the Gang's All Here."

Look out, men, the police — bang! bang! Tear gas bombs. Close the doors quick. Policemen in helmets with gas masks on. Why did they fire on us? Where did they come from so sudden? They have broken the glass in the front door. Bang! Tear gas fired through the broken glass. Defend yourselves as best you can. Bring up those hoses. Come on, pickets. Stones, bottles, bricks, hinges, bolts flying through the air. Over goes a car. There goes another of our men. More tear gas. Smarting eyes. Look out for that riot gun. Bang! Bang! Ahead, men, they are retreating. More gunfire. It's terrible. Wild shouts and women crying for the safety of their loved ones.

Now all is quiet.

Jan. 12, 1937

All is quiet on Chevrolet Avenue. Streets are littered with refuse. Broken windows, dismantled cars — all leave their story of the

Associated Press

Striking General Motors workers hang effigies of "stool pigeons" during their sitdown strike.

night before. We men are pleased. The governor is in town. We are glad the state troopers and the National Guard are here. We have faith in them. Maybe we can trust them.

Feb. 11, 1937

Wish our man who carries the mail would come. Hope the guard doesn't stop him today. Here he comes and he is smiling. He has a newspaper. Here's the headline — Strike Is Settled. Thank God. At last we go home, Home Sweet Home. The boys have voted to accept the agreement and here comes Fisher No. 1 down the street — crowds of people flash lights, flags waving, banners, shaking hands. Will be home soon now, dear, and I've not deserted you after all.

The strike affected 60 plants and ended with GM's recognition of the United Auto Workers. O'Rourke's diary is in the Archives of Labor and Urban Affairs, Walter P. Reuther Library, Wayne State University.

1940 *'A new crop from the same acres'*

Michigan starts over again, one more time

In the late '30s and early '40s, more than eight million people found work with federal employment projects. The Works Progress Administration was created in 1935 and renamed the Work Projects Administration in 1939. Later, it was absorbed by the Federal Works Agency, which was terminated in 1942. Most workers in the programs built roads, bridges or parks but the program also employed artists and writers. Scorned by some people as "boondogglers" and "pencil leaners," writers wrote a guide to Michigan in 1940. In it, they wrestled with the question of Michigan's identity — and their own.

What sort of state is Michigan? What are Michigan people like? To answer these questions is no simple task, because the people who inhabit it have been molded and conditioned by a variety of circumstances that never prevailed elsewhere.

Michigan's place in the national contemporary scene has been won by a series of physical and tonal changes that have made the state not one, but many; have given it not one, but half-a-dozen histories, and have stroked a painting that at today's point in its development is one of a fascinating, complicated character.

Today we know that the grand old days of the state's lumber prosperity — the Holy-Old-Mackinaw, Come-and-Get-It era, which reached its peak in the '80s — were days to be bitterly regretted. A whole section of the state was laid to waste and a great segment of its population forced to back up, make a new start.

During the period roughly paralleling the rise of logging to its climax, Michigan produced half the copper mined in the United States.

And then, almost before Michigan knew it, the greatest of the copper mines petered out, scores of iron workings were abandoned as no longer profitable in yield, and thousands of families, some of them foreign born, more of them second-generation Americans, were left with no place to go.

The plow could and would follow the ax, we determined; the farm would absorb those legions no longer needed in the forests and in the bowels of our earth. Michigan still winces when it thinks of that period: of those desperate, foolhardy campaigns to make agricultural centers of sawmill and mining towns.

People scrambled to get along in the slackness following pioneer booms — a people with a wide range of opportunities and obligations. But a people shifting from this to that, pulling chestnuts out of the fire and constantly starting over again cannot evolve a statewide type.

And then came Ford. And Chalmers and Olds. And Joy and Durant, Nash, Willys and Chapin. And Detroit became today's Detroit!

Detroit had created and perfected the assembly line. Detroit had blazed a trail for industry that was going to revolutionize industrial practice, and maybe society itself, before its influence was spent.

Dynamic Detroit, in the beginning of its rebirth so foreign, so hostile, to the balance of the state, gave to the state the one tool with which its greatest number of acres could be made to yield. The motorcar made the tourist industry what it is today.

We do not believe there is danger of our becoming a race of innkeepers. We have been through too much, we Michiganders, to let ourselves become servile or unctuous. We pump gas and hand out hot dogs and dig fish worms for a fee, yes. But we brought the pine down the Saginaw and Muskegon and all our

Detroit Institute of Arts

A WPA artist sketches other workers for a WPA arts project. WPA workers did everything from construction work to entertainment and the arts.

other rivers for a fee. And we went down into the earth after copper and iron for a fee. And we grow food and clothing for a fee, too. This selling of vacations has its roots in the same substance: in the soil. We are growing and marketing a new crop from the same acres that grew pine and hardwood and that blanketed our minerals, but we have come to respect, almost revere, those acres; we know they must not be abused and betrayed if they are to sustain us.

Easy come, easy go . . . Well, we know that now. We tried the easy way and met disaster. Now we are on the hard road, but we believe it is a high road. We Michigan folks are proud of what we are doing and the way we are doing it. We want the world to know of that pride, and by it we want to be known ourselves.

From "Michigan: A Guide to the Wolverine State," Oxford University Press, New York, 1941: pages 3-12.

Arsenal of democracy

"Our front employment office looks like the baggage room of Grand Central Station. Mr. Brown told me that we had 500 coming from Kentucky tomorrow and what was he to do with them. . . . And we expect to hire or try to hire some 55,000 more workers. We need 30,000 more right now."
— Josephine Gomon

1942 '150 families of squatters'

The rush for wartime jobs creates instant slums

Thousands of people drawn to the Detroit area by factory jobs during World War II had to scramble to find even ramshackle housing. In 1942, architect Alan Mather described the politics behind Detroit's wartime housing market.

Along the railroads going northward and just beyond the (Detroit) boundaries, in Warren Township, are new factories with a maximum employment capacity of 28,000. Near them are hundreds of newly built cottages. Inasmuch as Warren Township is still a farming community, farmer legislation prevails: Backhouses are permitted and a home is ready for occupancy even though the widely spaced and bent studs of its exterior are uncovered by wallboard or plaster. Foundations consist of concrete block piers resting on topsoil. Wells, drilled in a hurry, are just as quickly condemned by the State Board of Health and people are driving miles to public fountains with milk cans, garbage pails, oil cans and other assorted containers.

Ypsilanti, 28 miles west of the center of Detroit and near the Ford bomber plant, is rapidly turning into one big dormitory for the plant's employes. Strive as they may, citizens of this quiet teacher-training center don't seem to be able to prevent this change. For workers are making relatively good money and the best way to get it is to convert an old place into a rooming house. Evictions of people with families, in order to make such alterations, are a daily occurrence. Walking from the center of the town and out along Michigan Avenue for about four miles, I counted 135 trailers, some in twos and threes in farmhouse yards, others compactly ranged in rows in camps. Nearer the factory is an orchard from which 150 families of squatters, most of them bomber plant

Courtesy Alan Mather

Alan Mather in 1942

employes, were evicted in August. County health authorities in investigating found many drinking polluted water. There was an outbreak of a form of dysentery among the tenants and the state authorities felt compelled to evict them. A number of these wretched people purchased lots in nearby areas but were forbidden to build on them by the health department. The land had been found so low, water level so near the surface, that neither privies nor septic tanks could be erected without causing pollution of wells nearby.

The new factories in the suburbs were built for permanence. This worries local real estate investors. The opening of new residential areas would further depress

Associated Press

Two families lived in this tarpaper-covered shack near Willow Run in 1943.

values at the center. They were confronted by the threat of construction of *permanent* housing in industrial suburbs all over the country. And they resolved to have no such construction.

When looking at the Chrysler Tank Arsenal or the vast Ford bomber plant, miles from any built-up community, one is likely to be amazed at this opposition and its delaying tactics. "Where are the workmen going to live?" was the obvious question during the construction. But as day followed day and no permanent housing was built, the shortage of critical materials and increasing congestion in existing houses made it clear that only one kind of housing *could* be provided — barracks.

The real estate people in Detroit have never opposed barracks. Ford favors barracks. The UAW-CIO, which favored permanent housing to the last moment of the delaying battle, now favors temporary housing. They will get barracks. Two-hundred-seventy-two-thousand persons will move into Detroit between July 1942 and June 1943. Conditions are desperate. Time has been on the side of the righteous.

Mather, a native of Scotland, was 35 years old when he wrote this article. He worked as an architectural draftsman and job captain for various architectural firms until 1979. From the December, 1942 Pencil Points, courtesy Reinhold Publishing: pages 69-74.

1943 '500 coming from Kentucky'

Arriving workers overrun housing at Willow Run

As a Depression-era aide to Frank Murphy in his days as mayor and then governor, Josephine Gomon helped hundreds of people when there was not enough work to go around. In 1943, when the problem was too many jobs, she worked for the Ford Motor Co., lining up housing for the thousands of workers streaming into the Willow Run Bomber Plant. In letters to her children, she described the reception many new workers found.

March 10

Unless one has had the actual experience it would be difficult to picture the scene at Willow Run these days. Some of our employment staff has been around various parts of the country recruiting workers. These men and women arrive with their bags and baggage. They go through the routine and get hired in. Then they want to know where they are going to find a place to live. The government housing project called Willow Run Lodge opened about three weeks ago with a few rooms which have been expanded until some 550 are available and occupied. Also we sent a whole squad of plant protection men out to canvass the small towns — Ypsilanti, Ann Arbor, Northville, Plymouth, Milan, etc. — from door to door to beg the residents to make extra rooms available. About 300 rooms were added thus to our list.

Our front employment office looks like the baggage room of Grand Central Station. Mr. Brown told me that we had 500 coming from Kentucky tomorrow and what was he to do with them. They have been hired and are taking the train tomorrow. Well, it is a problem. And we expect to hire or try to hire some 55,000 more workers. We need 30,000 more right now.

Josephine Gomon had to find housing for hundreds of new arrivals a day.

June 4

We have recently adopted a policy of paying transportation for new workers being recruited in different districts around the country. The bunch to arrive yesterday came from Kentucky and were the first arrivals under the new arrangement. When they got here it was discovered that they had brought no money.

It is simple to know what happened. In mass hiring it is bound to happen. The fellows would ask about housing and food

Free Press photos

Barracks-style housing near the plant filled up as soon as it was built.

and Leo Dunn would say, "That's all taken care of at the office." Meaning that we now have places to put people. But they would interpret it to mean that they didn't have to pay for it. Well, we have no way of advancing funds until they are earned. So these fellows were up against it. They threatened to go back and Brown in the employment office thought that was the solution. "If they haven't got enough brains to know they have to have enough money to eat and sleep, they won't be much good anyway." Of course, they hadn't had a bite to eat all day. Besides which, they had stood up on a day coach for eight hours during the night, arriving Thursday morning.

So the next morning I called Mr. Miller at Rouge and met him at Willow Run and asked what they intended to do. Brown kept coming back to the fact that the men had been told to bring $35 until I thought I would go wild. In the middle of the discussion, the bus station called to say that there was a bunch of people from Kentucky there and what should they do with them. Brown said their fares were paid to Detroit — they would get to Willow Run by bus. I said, "You

guaranteed their fares to Willow Run. Seventy-five cents means a lot to these people." Brown said, "We did not. We paid their fares to Detroit. They can get here as best they can." I picked up the guarantee and it said, "To Ypsilanti Willow Run Plant."

So I wrote a paragraph that one of the conditions of being hired was that they were to have $35 in their pockets when they arrived and it was incorporated in the letter of agreement that they had to sign. We tore up the previous copies and had a thousand new ones printed right away.

The people at the bus station, and thousands more who came after them, found work at the plant. Gomon was not so lucky. She returned from vacation in October 1945 to find a note on her desk telling her she had been fired in a shakeup at Ford Motor Co. A longtime figure in Detroit politics, she died in 1975. From the Josephine Gomon papers, box one, in the Michigan Historical Collections at the University of Michigan's Bentley Historical Library.

1943 *'The tempo of Detroit life'*

British envoy deplores crowding, prices and women's slacks

Arthur Bray was working at the British Consulate in Detroit during World War II when he wrote this report on city life in July 1943. Bray was writing a month after race riots on June 20 and 21. That summer, shoes, canned goods, meat, butter and cheese were being rationed. A top song was "Mairzy Doats," and "Casablanca" won the Oscar for best motion picture.

Starting in 1941, the war gradually and increasingly affected the tempo of Detroit life. As the recent race riots seem to have marked some kind of high point in this change, this would appear to be a good time to survey it.

The main visible changes have been in prices, in the crowding, in the large-scale employment of women and in the 24-hour nature of employment and social life.

In Detroit there are not enough policemen, and hardly any Negro policemen at all, in spite of the huge colored population. It has also meant a very rapid turnover in the types of labor that get low pay, such as laundry, hotel and restaurant workers.

Life has been visibly changed by prices and wages, but they have not made a very deep change in the style of living. It is a question of degree rather than kind. However, the employment of women in very large numbers, in a town where two years ago there was hardly a single female industrial worker, has had, and will have, a profound effect on society as a whole. It has doubled or tripled the income in many families, especially in the lower class. Having each spouse on a separate shift, quite apart from the independence conferred by separate earnings, has led to separations in social life and amusements which seem likely to be permanent in some cases.

An aspect of the war which is very obnoxious to everyone is the crowding, in public places, on the street, in transport, in parks, lifts, shops and places of amusement. You are jostled in trams by fat women, fall over children, have men in greasy clothing sit on your lap and their female counterparts hold on to your sleeve to stand up.

The crowding extends to all housing, but particularly to Negroes. Various forms of discrimination drive them into those small areas where they can afford the rent; they are invariably overcharged. The whites try to get near their factories, now that petrol is short, and crowd into areas never meant to hold them, where sewage and water facilities are primitive in the extreme. The latter may suit the hillbillies, but even they have never had to live crowded together. The old Middle Western expansiveness and open attitude to strangers shows very worn at the edges.

(Spending) is flamboyant only in the amount spent and not in the manner or in the quality offered. Spirits and beer form the chief backbone of the purchases, but dancing, all-night bowling, nightclubs of the cheaper sort and movies of all sorts take another portion.

The majority of the masses are just not interested in the war or its possibilities. The speed and tension of the work has something to do with this, but the money interest has the most. So many are in a new form of life, with money they never had before, that they are in a whirl and cannot find their feet. They have swept the more stolid locals with them. Some of the more amusing symptoms show in clothing fashions. One sees females in slacks of all kinds and shapes. Coats and ties are worn by men less and less. In the mobs that churned around the shopping center on the

Free Press photo

The crowd at Detroit's Fox Theater was well dressed for "Coney Island" in 1945.

memorable 21st of June, there was not a single jacket to be seen. (Much of the violence occurred along storefronts on Hastings Street, the center of Detroit's black community in the 1940s. It is now I-375.) Formal dress is very rare. Much personal decoration has become flamboyant in the extreme, vivid ties and sham jewelry with "plenty diamonds" leading the van. The apogee: the zoot suit, which, as a matter of fact, has not been very popular here.

So much for what one sees. The significance is another matter. If it were a normal town, the various types of social disturbance which are so obvious would spell its decay and ruin in the first month after the war. But this is not called Dynamic Detroit for nothing. Few towns have had such a growth, from 250,000 population at the turn of the century to some two millions now.

Its population predominantly consider themselves citizens of other places and the apathy of the workers to the outside world, considering the hundred million tons of shipping that has always been theirs, is nothing short of astounding.

Another boom or another Depression can make no difference. In the Depression you can go and live in another town, where your family is, probably, and you have no responsibility and no cares. You can go back when the work picks up and lead your own life on your own money, and your machines will turn out more than anyone else, and faster, and better. If you have to feed the starving foreigners, well and good, you have money. If you have not, you will not be in Detroit for long anyway. So why worry about the morrow?

Bray's report was reprinted with Thomas E. Hachey's "Detroit in July, 1943," in the Winter, 1975 issue of Michigan History magazine: pages 227-238.

1943 'Duds, and some characters'

She's in the Army now: Librarian joins WACs

It was 1943 when Detroit librarian Anna Moore, then in her mid-30s, joined the Women's Army Corps. In her diary, she wrote about life as a WAC at Keesler Field in Biloxi, Miss.

Dec. 6

This was the day. Reported to the Army for active duty. The Detroit group gathered at the railroad station to travel together to Grand Rapids, from where we take off for Daytona Beach, excited and nervous and a little scared. This community living is going to be something new for me. And it will be the first time I've ever been away from home when I couldn't go back any time I wished. Hard to say goodby to the family. If Mother had bawled, so would I. Thank God she didn't. Now, after a short train trip, in a hotel room in Grand Rapids, sharing a bed with a gal I never saw before.

Dec. 9

Arrived Daytona Beach 1 p.m. Met by huge bus, which took us to cantonment area. Assigned to Co. 2, 5th regiment. One-hundred-fifty women from Michigan, Illinois, Wisconsin and Iowa. Speeches by company officers. Non-commissioned officers introduced. Beds assigned — very close quarters. First lesson in bed making. First experience with mess hall. Food better than expected. Amenities lacking. Well, did I expect tablecloths, napkins and silver? Nope — and I didn't get them.

Dec. 13

Sunday. Day of rest and gladness. All kinds of women; all kinds of backgrounds. Pretty good bunch for the most part. Some obvious duds, and some characters: Grandma Yankes, 45, from southern Illinois, works harder than anybody else and quotes the Bible continually. Two sons in service.

Burton Historical Collection, Detroit Public Library
Anna Moore in uniform

Kelly, blond show girl, reputed to be former striptease artist. Grant, about my age, cultured, traveled, intelligent — interesting person to be with. Boots, wholesome, practical, good-looking and competent. Murphy, MacAvoy, Myers in my rank. Young and fun and full of the devil. Toby, former doctor's office clerk. Edith, farm gal from Iowa; all kinds.

Dec. 14

Army sanitation — careful instructions about keeping clean; in practice I never have time to wash my hands between 6 a.m. and 6 p.m. unless I skip mail call. Every time I get near a latrine or washroom, the whistle blows to fall in for something else. Seem to

Free Press photo

WACs march down Woodward Avenue on Oct. 19, 1943.

be continually changing clothes: fatigues before breakfast, Class A after cleaning, fatigues again for (physical training), class A for retreat. Five minutes to change each time. When I get back home, I expect I will be arrested for indecent exposure. I can see myself coming home from work and as I go up the front steps taking off this and unbuttoning that. I am usually undressed by the time I reach my own little six feet of floor.

Nothing too difficult about this Army business. They make the rules and you play the way they say — while they are around. Any personal modifications you can achieve without detection are just so much velvet. Whole thing is accepting it as such and not kicking against the obvious stupidities.

Moore served 27 months in the Army before returning to her library job. When she died at age 45 in 1952, she was assistant librarian at the Burton Historical Collection, Detroit Public Library, where this diary is kept.

1944 'I won't have any friends left'

War stories are delivered in pen pal's letters

World War II was far from Detroit, but Esther Madejczyk had a close-up look at the Pacific Theater in letters from the more than 20 soldiers with whom she corresponded. Pvt. Norman Borchman of Detroit wrote these letters.

Nov. 21, 1944

It's beginning to turn bad, but we can't kick since we are doing a fine job. Work is just about the same and everything in general is fine, but it won't be for long, so you just have to read between the lines of what I'm trying to say and hope we all pull through all right.

Esther, I was glad to hear from you again, but your letter wasn't a cheerful one as the others. Have you heard any more of Ed? I had two cousins killed in action, one in France and one in Italy. Letters from home tell me of many deaths and wounded. Looks as if I come through all this, I won't have any friends left home. I often wonder how I will come out. I don't worry, but it gets you thinking of what is ahead of you, not knowing from one minute to the next. I still haven't lost my courage, and I went through plenty, but what is coming next will be much more worse.

Feb. 2, 1945

We are in the Philippines and have been on the go ever since we arrived here. In less than four weeks we have moved six times on trucks and dusty roads. We are now set up in the city (in) what used to be the slums, and still is. The best part of the city is all in ruin and nothing to see, so you have a good idea of just where I'm at.

When we knew we were coming to the Philippines, we had in our minds that when we arrived here it would be like home, going to nightclubs and theaters, but it was just

Courtesy Esther Brockmiller

Esther Madejczyk and Norman Borchman at Frankenmuth in 1947.

another dream. There isn't a building left.

I'm unable to mention what the Japanese did to the civilians and their babies, and furthermore maybe it's best not to. All I can say (is) it's horrible and hate to think of it. Many people died and are dying from hunger. The city simply stinks and is sickening. The civilians have no place to bury the dead, so they bury them between the walk and the street.

The 50 centavo isn't any good now and the Filipinos are giving them away for

Free Press photo
The same Detroit street corner seen in the picture on Page 171, but the date is Aug. 14, 1945 — VJ Day.

souvenirs.

Esther, thank you for the cute picture. You both look as if you were fairies with those gowns on that large lawn.

Borchman died in the mid '70s in Montreal, his last stop on an around-the- *world trip. Esther Madejczyk married Harry Brockmiller Jr. in 1973, and retired from IBM after working there 32 years. From the World War II Correspondence file at the Burton Historical Collection, Detroit Public Library.*

1947 'Women did nearly all the work'

Automobile manufacturers retool to build the tools of war

Detroit's automobile plants were the heart of the "Arsenal of Democracy" during World War II. Shortly after the war, Chrysler Corp. recounted its role in the Allied fight in a small book, "Great Engines and Great Planes."

Because cars and planes both are made of metals and powered by the same type of engines, there had been loose talk when war first threatened of how, by a simple twist of the wrist, the assembly lines which turned out automobiles in the millions would produce planes, at once and in nearly comparable numbers.

The drastic difference is that an automobile is a utility and a convenience, while any military plane is a weapon. If your weapon is not better than your competitor's — the enemy — your customer will die, your product will be destroyed. At any cost of money or time, therefore, the design must be improved daily, hourly.

A secondary difference between cars and planes in 1940 lay in quantities. Until then, aircraft had been built a few at a time. Ten ships was a good order, 100 a stroke of fortune. The Glenn L. Martin Co., a leader in this field and founded before World War I, had not yet built a thousand planes, fewer units than Chrysler was being asked to make on its first order.

DeSoto-Warren quickly discovered that it would be best to dimension all Martin "lofts" (patterns) both for its own use and that of its subcontractors. Here was another striking contrast in methods. A loft is more like a dressmaker's pattern than a blueprint. It is concerned primarily with contours, is not dimensioned. To Detroit tool men, they were as freakish as a Vogue dinner gown pattern. A new drafting department had to be set up in the Chrysler Engineering Division to detail these lofts into a language understood by automotive men.

• • •

Another Chrysler assignment in the nation's aircraft production program came in January 1942. This time, Curtiss-Wright Co. asked the corporation to take on the job of building the center wing panel — the foundation structure — of the Navy's fastest, strongest and biggest dive bomber of the recent war — the Helldiver.

The right half of this panel was assigned to the DeSoto division, the left to the Chrysler division. The company's Highland Park plant was called on to provide some of the stampings, with important machining work turned over to Plymouth. To the Dodge Aluminum Forge went the task of providing many of the forgings.

• • •

With labor chronically short in Detroit, the percentage of women workers on the Helldiver rose to 69 overall. In some departments, women did nearly all the work; even in machining, forging and stamping, they formed half or more of the labor force.

• • •

Chrysler-Jefferson finished its 5,723d and last left wing on the day the atomic bomb fell on Hiroshima. A few right-wing panels still were in course of assembly at DeSoto when Japan's capitulation terminated the contract five days later.

From Wesley Scot, "Great Engines and Great Planes," Chrysler Corp., Detroit, 1947: pages 101-123.

Chrysler Corp.

Women on the job at the Jefferson plant. In some departments, nearly all of the workers were women.

On the move

"One only has to look at the manifests of some of these small ships that are coming into the Great Lakes to see that there is no limit to the variety of products that can be brought by ship, ranging from paper, wood pulp, clay products, beer and liquor to even tulip bulbs from Holland."
— Foster Winter

Courtesy Thomas Andrew Sykora

Thomas Andrew Sykora
aboard the steamer Colonel in
1950.

1946 'A great wind hit us'

17-year-old cabin boy rides out a wild one

Thomas Andrew Sykora of Lakewood, Ohio, was a 17-year-old cabin boy in 1946, spending his second summer on the Great Lakes. Sykora worked aboard the freighter Marquette and ended each day by writing in his diary.

June 19

Up the Detroit River and past Detroit at 5 p.m. The mail boat brought me one letter. The sun is out and it's a beautiful day. There is still a stiff breeze. In Lake St. Clair, a beautiful yacht kept following us broadside. Listened to the (Joe) Louis-(Billy) Conn fight.

June 21

We passed through the Straits of Mackinac about 1 a.m. I slept through the whistling, which is done every time we pass a light. The icebreaker Mackinac passed our stern early this morning. The lake is very choppy. There is a very stiff wind.

June 22

Entered the "door" — on the way into Green Bay — at 5:30 p.m. Went to eat, and after I finished I walked out on deck when all of a sudden a great wind hit us. In the bay it got so bad the boat was rolling to a 30-degree angle. We had to put all the clamps on the hatches. The assistant engineer said it was the worst storm he had seen in years. The captain had two wheelsmen up there trying to get our course. They had the rudder turned for 20 minutes, but it wouldn't budge the boat. It just made the whole ship go sideways. When we got opposite Escanaba, we turned and followed the storm right into the breakwall. The waves were so high they broke on deck even though we were going light. That was the worst rolling I've ever seen on a ship of this size. One porter started to whistle to get the storm off his mind.

When the captain heard him, he told him to stop but Fred thought he was kidding. There's a superstition that if you whistle during a storm it will bring more wind. You shouldn't whistle at all, anyway.

June 24

The rain stopped at 9 a.m. and they began to load the ore. It's in real big chunks, easy to unload.

June 26

Arrived at Toledo at 12 noon and slept until 3 in the afternoon, then walked around the C&O docks there. Didn't do much at all on my watch. Got unloaded at 6:30 and had to wait an hour for the Joliet to get loaded before we could move into position.

June 27

Left Toledo at 6 a.m. The shoveling and rinsing down was pretty tough. One reason was lack of sleep, I guess. Two automobile carriers were on their way to some Lake Erie port. They're nice-looking boats with deckloads of new shiny automobiles.

June 29

Woke up in a cold room this morning. There is a terrible fog. They've been blowing that whistle every day. At some times we couldn't even see the midships. It's like a heavy smoke. They kept her blowing although we didn't hear one other ship all day. I heard over the ship radio that there are a lot of ships anchored in Whitefish Bay waiting to enter the locks.

Sykora spent his career dispatching and directing operations of Great Lakes vessels. Today he is an officer in the Great Lakes Historical Society, living in Rocky River, Ohio, and writing a book on the passenger steamer Put-in-Bay. From Inland Seas magazine, April 1947: pages 77-80.

1946 *'Shopping should be made easy'*

Grand Rapids architect foresees modern shopping centers

In 1946, Kenneth C. Welch of Grand Rapids described a revolutionary plan to bring stores together into "shopping centers" on the fringes of cities. At the time, Walter Reuther was the new president of the United Automobile Workers, box-office stars were Bing Crosby, Ingrid Bergman and Humphrey Bogart and "The Gypsy" spent 20 weeks on the Hit Parade.

We have just observed, with great fanfare and beating of the publicist's drums, the 50th anniversary of the motorcar. The anniversary in itself is not important, for age is not always a criterion of social impact, but the motorcar, from its very inception, ground into oblivion much of our pre-conceived formulas for living and commerce.

In those 50 years since the first automobile went hesitatingly down the first highway, social changes have also come into being. Most people now work less, earn more, relax more, go more places, do more things and buy more merchandise. Primarily, they have expanded their method of living so that shopping for daily and even seasonal needs no longer necessitates an occasional trip downtown.

In a well-designed commercial area, shopping should be made easy. Today, women are forced to shop in areas built around main thoroughfares, where street crossings are not only dangerous but a definite deterrent to pedestrian traffic.

The automobile parking problem is a serious one in every city and town in the country. The automobile has been so suddenly superimposed upon the existing rigid municipal pattern — which just happened to fit the horse and buggy and to partially fit the streetcar. (Cities have not) been able to catch up with the rapidly changing transportation habits or the social

Michigan Historical Collections, University of Michigan

Kenneth C. Welch

structure brought on by the war.

Apart from the problem of the downtown shopping area is the neighborhood, that droplet of humanity in the peripheral of the city.

Perhaps the solution lies in bringing a greater number of products and services to the people rather than expecting the people to come to them. The planned shopping center in all city planning to come is perhaps the most exciting prospect.

Here, on land not expensive but close to where people live, will grow a center that will have a branch of the city's big department store with its wide regional appeal. It will also have a drugstore, supermarket, theater, hardware store, variety store, shoe store and

The Northland Shopping Center as it looked in the 1950s when it was new.

all those myriad of retail operations which fulfill the seasonal as well as the daily needs of a growing population. Parking space will be provided amply and conveniently because land cost will permit it and common sense will dictate it.

Automotive traffic to and from the places where people work and to their homes will be vital to its success. It will be close enough to dwelling places to permit easy walking. It will be on transportation routes to permit those who live too far to walk to get there quickly, either with or without using their own cars.

It will be clean and fresh and all-inviting, with much of the natural surroundings left untouched to provide a pleasant atmosphere. It will, by its very alertness to the community need and its modern approach, become the neighborhood's answer to an automobile-choked downtown.

Welch, an architect and planner, helped design one of the nation's first regional shopping centers in Framingham, Mass., and later worked on Northland in Soutfieldand Breton Village in Grand Rapids. Before he died in 1973, he saw his idea remake the face of American cities. Reprinted with permission from the July, 1946, issue of American Druggist, a Hearst Business Publication.

1953 *'The risk of losing the entire deal'*

Mackinac Bridge hurdles its last obstacle

It took years of studies and tests to settle engineering challenges to a bridge across the Straits of Mackinac, but the plan ran into a tougher challenge in 1953 — a year-end deadline to arrange financing. Without it, the bridge was likely doomed to failure. The financial tightrope walk unfolded in the Mackinac Bridge Authority's minutes, kept by authority Secretary Lawrence A. Rubin.

Jan. 8

(Investment banker Bernard J.) Van Ingen stated that in his best professional opinion ($96 million) of bonds could be sold. His firm would be ready to do so by April 1, 1953. He pointed out that it would require a tremendous amount of hard work on the part of all concerned, but he was confident it could be successfully accomplished.

May 1

(Chairman Prentiss M.) Brown pointed out that he and (Vice-chairman Charles T.) Fisher had had a meeting with representatives of several investment houses and had been unofficially told that without some state or federal subsidy, or the faith and credit of the state backing the revenue bonds, it was unlikely that they would be marketable.

June 3

Chairman Brown raised the question as to whether the authority should proceed now to market the bonds for the proposed bridge in view of current market conditions, or wait until fall for possible improvement. Mr. Van Ingen's advice was requested and he pointed out that waiting involved many hazards. He stated that there was a tremendous amount of financing scheduled for the near future and that delay of the Mackinac Bridge issue would be (forced) to

H.D. Ellis

Workers check cable diameter during compacting operations near the top of the south tower in 1957.

compete with this financing.

June 18

Mr. Brown stated that Mr. Van Ingen had been quite optimistic and confident right up until Tuesday afternoon that the sale could have been completed as planned.

Mr. Brown related that according to Mr. Van Ingen, offerings of tax-exempt bonds scheduled for sale in the next 30 days, plus generally poor market conditions, caused potential buyers of Mackinac Bridge bonds to hold back. Mr. Van Ingen reported to Mr. Brown Wednesday night that he had orders for $33 million but did not want to gamble on trying to push through the remaining $63 million at the risk of losing the entire deal. (At this point, the authority decided to postpone the bond sale.)

Nov. 24

Mr. Brown, Mr. Fisher and your

Free Press Files

The bridge's towers were erected first, then cables were hung. The roadway was built last.

secretary met with (investment banker James S.) Abrams in New York on Nov. 11, 1953. Mr. Abrams pointed out that he had offered to co-operate with Van Ingen & Co. in financing the bridge, but was told (he) was free to approach the authority with his own plan.

Mr. Abrams then revealed that his idea for financing the structure was to issue $76 million of four-percent, first-lien bonds and $20 million of second-lien revenue bonds. The total interest costs on such a plan would be the same as a $96-million, 4¼-percent issue.

Dec. 17

The secretary reported that he had received a sealed bid prior to 10 a.m. of Dec. 17, 1953, shortly before the meeting began. It stated that a management group had bid

an interest rate of four percent on the authority's offering of $79.8 million, (reflecting rising costs) of Series A bonds, and 5¼ percent on the authority's offering of Series B bonds. No other bids were received.

The bid was accepted and, except for a few technicalities, all that remained was for Rubin to sign 99,800 bonds. Even with the help of a 10-pen signature device, it took him the better part of three days. The bridge opened to traffic on Nov. 1, 1957. Rubin is the author of "Bridging the Straits," published by Wayne State University Press in 1985. From the Mackinac Bridge Authority papers, box one, in the Michigan Historical Collections at the University of Michigan's Bentley Historical Library.

1953 *'I would snap it up without delay'*

Merchandising man sees bargain in St. Lawrence Seaway

In 1953, the U.S. House of Representatives' Committee on Public Works held hearings on whether to join Canada in a project to turn the St. Lawrence River into a seaway that would open the Great Lakes to ocean-going vessels. In Washington hearings on June 17, 1953, J.L. Hudson Co. Treasurer Foster Winter argued in support of the project.

As a merchandising man, I think I know something about the impact of the cost of transportation upon the price of the final product to the customer. We in J.L. Hudson import a large amount of merchandise from all over the world, and I can assure you that direct water transportation to Detroit by the St. Lawrence Seaway would save almost one-half the transportation cost of the materials we import. I know that the opponents of this project have a way of ridiculing the kind of products that may be imported. One only has to look at the manifests of some of these small ships that are coming into the Great Lakes to see that there is no limit to the variety of products that can be brought by ship, ranging from paper, wood pulp, clay products, beer and liquor to even tulip bulbs from Holland.

I recently had something to do with the establishment of a $25-million shopping center in suburban Detroit (Northland). Before committing ourselves to this enterprise, we of course made studies of the retail sales potential of the area. That included population trends, income levels and shopping habits, and we are confident that our commitment will be justified by the public response, as all the space has been committed.

Now our commitment in that one shopping center is more than 25 percent of the commitment that this committee is being asked to make on a reimbursable investment basis. This St. Lawrence Canal is going to serve a shopping area containing 50 million people, with income, depending upon the number of states in the area, of from $60 billion to $75 billion, and retail sales of $30 billion to $40 billion a year. If the ($100 million) investment in this seaway is not justified, certainly the investment of the New York Central roadbed and rolling stock serving this area is not justified, or the investment in highway and trucking lines serving this area is not justified. A market area that is good enough for these hardheaded businessmen, anxious and eager to serve this rich market, is certainly good enough for a commitment of about $100 million for this canal.

I take it that our forward-looking and hardheaded, business-minded Canadian friends have come to that conclusion, and regardless of what this committee does they are ready to proceed. I understand, however, that as a friendly gesture our neighbors have left the door ajar for us to participate, provided we don't delay their plans. Gentlemen, if I had a good business proposition such as this, with friends who are willing to discuss a partnership participation, I would snap it up without delay.

The United States eventually joined Canada in building the seaway and it opened in 1959, raising vessels more than 600 feet on their trip from the Atlantic Ocean to Lake Superior. From "Hearings Before the Committee on Public Works, House of Representatives, on House Joint Resolution 104," U.S. Government Printing Office, Washington, D.C., 1953: pages 402-410.

Free Press files

The S.S. North American follows the S.S. South American in the seaway's Dwight D. Eisenhower Lock.

Foster Winter

1956 *'I have to make every penny count'*

Everyday concerns spill out of senator's mailbag

In 1956, Elvis Aaron Presley's "Heartbreak Hotel" became a top single, General Motors President Harlowe Curtice was Time magazine's Man of the Year and Dwight Eisenhower beat Adlai Stevenson for the presidency. The everyday concerns of Detroiters were reflected in their letters to Democratic Sen. Cora Brown, the nation's first black woman state senator.

This letter is a request that you may do all in your power to uphold the bills now coming up in the Legislature dealing with tests of drunkenness by the drunkometer.

It has long been my contention that the majority of accidents are caused by drivers either having had one drink or enough to leave no doubt as to their condition.

Since one drink does for the youth unaccustomed to larger amounts of liquor as much damage to the ability as four to the seasoned driver, there is no sense in measuring abilities lost by bottles or glasses.

The drunkometer test would settle that.
Highland Park

I am writing you concerning Bill No. 1068 and wish you could give it your full support.

I am a widow with very limited means and I do not feel that it is in any way fair to have merchants restrict goods on sale to buyers.

I have to make every penny count, and when fruit juices, fruits, butter, eggs, flour, sugar, bacon and shortenings are on sale I like to stock up, as I do all our own baking.

I am a long way from the markets and have no car, and to walk way over and receive the short reply, "One to a customer," it's a near-unnecessary trip.
Detroit

The Detroit metropolitan area needs a university where students can obtain an education while earning a living.

Free Press files
Cora M. Brown was the first black woman in the nation to be elected state senator.

Wayne University has served this need in the past but must expand to meet the increasing demands on its facilities. The Detroit Board of Education is unable to finance this expansion.

The most logical solution to the problem is the transfer of the university to the state of Michigan.
Highland Park

I am 12 years old and live in your district. I attend Hampton School and have been chosen the captain of the affirmative in a coming debate on whether Michigan should or shouldn't have capital punishment.

I would be much obliged if you would send me some information on what has come up in the Senate and the Legislature on the subject since you have been serving.
Detroit

Senate Bill 1068 would have forbidden merchants from placing limits on goods sold for less than their cost and never came to a final vote. Breath tests are now commonplace when drunken driving is suspected, Wayne University is now Wayne State, and Michigan continues to debate capital punishment. Brown, a former Detroit police officer, served from 1953 to 1957. She died in 1972 at age 58. From the Cora M. Brown papers, box one, the Burton Historical Collection, Detroit Public Library.

1960 *'They flew to sure destruction'*

A Duck Island diary reflects issues great and small

Chase Salmon Osborn, Michigan's governor in 1911-1912, began corresponding with Stella Lee Brunt in 1921 and three years later, they met. They began working together in 1927 and Osborn, married but legally separated from his wife, adopted Brunt in 1931 so she could live and travel with him. At the time, he was 71, she was 37 and he gave her the name Stellanova. On April 9, 1949, with Osborn gravely ill, they had the adoption annulled and were married. Two days after their wedding,

Osborn died. He was 89. She continued to refer to him in her diary as "Dearest." Eleven years after his death, she took a respite from her work as an activist for a world union of democracies to visit the camp they shared on Duck Island, near Sault Ste. Marie. In her diary, she wove an intricate pattern of past and future, that place and other places, her life and his.

Sept. 13

Did some small shopping. Bought a Motorola from Northern Electric so I could

Albany (N.Y.) Herald

Chase and Stellanova Osborn shortly before he died.

listen in on the UN this week at camp.

Then Mr. Leo LeLievre showed me the new armory and the sewage disposal plant on the land Dearest gave them on the St. Mary's. Then he took me to call on W.B. Robertson. His son, James, drove us out past the tannery building, now the property of the Algoma Steel Co. of Canada, and showed me the land and the development going on, dredging the channel, making new land, preparing dockage. Also he showed where the new international bridge will be begun in the next two weeks. I saw more of the Sault in a few hours than in the past 10 years.

Sept. 14

Tomorrow is the day I have come back for. Eleven years ago tomorrow, Dearest returned to his island for the last time, not ever, in our way of speaking, to leave again.

This is the day our two vaults were carried from the scow at the dock and set in place. One is conscious here, unescapably, that mankind flows in a constant stream, from birth to death, as individuals. The stream changes with the morphology of the Earth but, in general, goes on. Some of us, on the journey, catch and reflect a ray of the sun or the shadow of the cloud. The experience is miraculous. Mine continues here, a while, longer than I had expected. In what form, where, is the great spark that we knew as Chase Osborn?

Sept. 16

I ate lunch on the chaise lounge — great flat rock south of the cabin — with cushions to cover the hazelnut shells of the reigning squirrel, my head shaded by hazel bushes; but the southeast wind made it less than pleasant, even in the bright sun.

So begins our 12th year of being together — apart.

Surely (Soviet premier Nikita) Khrushchev does not plan to scuttle the UN, which is now so useful to him. Perhaps he wishes to scuttle the secretary general, and elect, or try to elect, one with more pigmentation in his skin? There are now 50 votes in Africa. Soon there will be 58, out of 108.

Oct. 4

That absolutely worthless Motorola cost, with tax, $32.24. I thought I paid $29 to hear the show of the century at the UN — the high point in this struggle to which I have given a decade of my life — it did not work.

The Sault paper says Khrushchev has renewed his attack on (UN Secretary General Dag) Hammarskjold, threatening to refuse to recognize UN decisions unless its machinery is revised. How long will it last?

Oct. 8

Fifteen beautiful goldeneyes, frightened of me, flew off to the head of the island straight into gunshot of hunters whose season had opened at noon. Afraid of something not to fear at all, they flew to sure destruction. The patriotic organizations (have) been following that course for more than 10 years, teaching Americans deathly fear of even discussing a pooling of sovereignty with other free people for fear of losing sovereignty and getting into a world federation; while we have been rapidly losing sovereignty to the communist dictatorship and the communist system of dictatorship has been rapidly organizing a world communist framework.

From the Stella Osborn papers, box 16, in the Michigan Historical Collections at the University of Michigan's Bentley Historical Library.

Into
the future

"*Man is just beginning to wonder,
still mustering the courage to dare
to challenge, much less explore,
the vast unknown . . .*"
— Tom Avery

1961 *'Michigan on the rocks'*

With state finances in ruins a political star rises

Readers of the Feb. 25, 1961, issue of the Saturday Evening Post turned to Harold H. Martin's cover story, "Michigan: The Problem State," and got a picture of a state caught in a political vise.

That glow which has been lighting the northern sky like the aurora borealis here of late is the face of the state of Michigan, red with anger, frustration and embarrassment.

The frustration stems from the fact that things have not been going well for the past few years in a state that has always been rich, proud and superbly confident of its destiny as one of the great industrial areas of the nation. Population growth seems to be leveling off, unemployment is rising, old industries are moving out or merging, and new businesses are not coming in in numbers great enough to keep the work force busy.

The anger is a product of the fierce family fight in which Michigan's citizens have been blaming one another for this sad state of affairs; the embarrassment stems from the realization that, throughout the acrimonious squabbling, the neighbors have been listening. Today, Michigan sorely fears, the rest of the nation believes what her own citizens have been saying about her — that high taxes, high wage rates and labor-loving courts have created a climate in which industry no longer feels comfortable, and that pigheaded partisan politics has got the state's finances into a fantastic mess.

The state is in the wrenching process of completing a great political transition. A quarter of a century ago, Democrats were as rare in Michigan as alligators, and they enjoyed about the same social standing. The state was solidly and complacently Republican, and stubbornly anti-union and pro-open shop. Today the state is almost evenly divided between Democrats and Republicans.

The hottest fights, naturally, raged around the nature of the tax program which should be passed to support Michigan's admittedly excellent state services. (Gov. G. Mennen) Williams, with the backing of labor, favored a graduated personal income tax and a tax on corporation profits. To the Republicans, this was a device of the devil — or of Walter Reuther, president of the United Auto Workers, which was worse — and they would have none of it. They favored, instead, legislation that would increase the state sales tax from three percent to four percent.

This controversy raged for a year, with the contestants butting heads like two bull elks with their antlers locked, neither side being willing to budge an inch.

Slowly, a huge state deficit built up. The word had spread that Michigan was broke, and wags in bars began ordering a new drink, "Michigan on the rocks."

Last December, Williams had to do some capitulating himself. The people, in a referendum, had approved a constitutional amendment approving a one-percent rise in the sales tax — on the purely human reasoning perhaps that, though an income tax must be paid in chunks, a sales tax is paid in dribbles and therefore is less painful. In December Williams somewhat morosely called the Legislature into special session for the purpose of legalizing this new tax.

Many surveys of the state's tax programs have been made in recent years by experts from both within and without the state. All agree that, if Michigan is to provide the services her people want, some form of income tax and corporation tax is inevitable.

After years of squabbling, the mood of the citizens at the moment is one of anger and impatience with both Democrats and

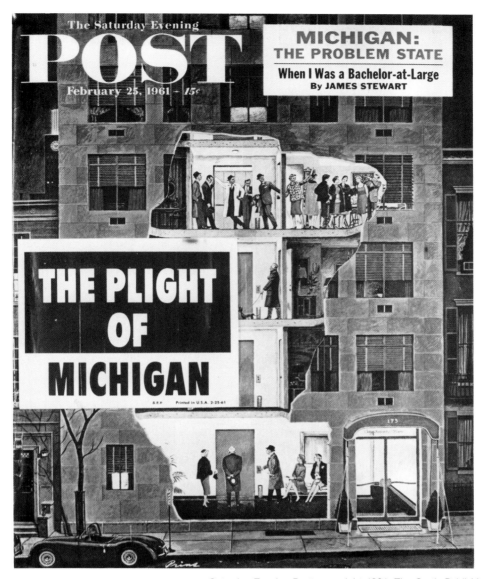

Saturday Evening Post, copyright 1961, The Curtis Publishing Co.

The cover of the Feb. 25, 1961 Saturday Evening Post

Republicans.

One prominent Michigander who has sensed the growing spread of this "a plague on both your houses" sentiment is trying to harness and redirect this discontent into useful channels. George Romney, president of American Motors, has organized a group called Citizens for Michigan, which brings together labor leaders, industrialists, Democrats, Republicans and independents dedicated to doing what they think is best for Michigan without regard to party or the labor-management struggle.

The group recently came out for flat-rate personal and corporate income taxes, a recommendation which did not endear Romney to his fellow industrialists.

Romney was elected governor in 1962. In 1967, under his administration, a tax revision was enacted calling for taxes on personal income, corporate income and the profits of financial institutions. From The Saturday Evening Post, copyright 1961, The Curtis Publishing Co., Feb. 21, 1961: pages 13-15 and 86-88.

1962 'People are becoming pessimistic'

Political wheeling and dealing rewrite state's constitution

As one of 144 delegates working in Lansing on a new state Constitution, Charles L. Follo, a Democrat from Escanaba, kept a frank diary of the 1962 proceedings and behind-the-scenes wrangling.

Feb. 6

A week ago I flew up to Escanaba via North Central Airlines to spend the weekend up there, and this weekend I spent in Kalamazoo at my brother's home. In each place, I found that many people are becoming pessimistic over the prospects of a good Constitution because of the political maneuvering of both parties. The political ambitions of George Romney and the possibility of his candidacy (for governor) have driven the Democrats frantic in their attempts to discredit him as a member of the convention and in other ways. With this I have little sympathy. In fact, I think they have brought him more publicity and have made themselves look foolish. I cannot go for such narrow partisanship.

March 27

Romney and Brake have compromised on the election vs. the appointment of the administrative board, on the 15-mill tax limitation and on earmarking of funds. In other words, it seems to me that Brake, by giving up a little, has gained much more and Romney has given up much of his idealistic program. The Democrats screamed to high heaven about "a deal" and threatened to walk out of the convention.

I have gotten so disgusted with caucuses that I do not attend very regularly. They seem to be conducted like CIO meetings and I am afraid that the CIO is dominating our caucus as they seem to dominate the Democratic party in Michigan.

Michigan Historical
Collections,
University of Michigan

Charles L. Follo
represented Escanaba.

June 2

Votes came so fast that we found it difficult to leave our seats lest we miss voting on a crucial issue. Many times issues were decided by one or two votes. We worked late hours. Sometimes we were there until as late as 12:30 a.m., when many of the delegates were exhausted and many dozed during the debates.

Before the vote of the convention on the final result, Bill Marshall sent Frank Perlich over to me to ask me to abstain. I told him that I could not abstain because it would be ridiculous to do that after working for 7½ months on a document that the taxpayers had sent me here to help make. Besides, in my opinion, while I am far from enthusiastic about it, the proposed Constitution represents at least a small improvement over the one we have now.

In the fall of 1962, Michigan voters elected Romney governor. On April 1, 1963, they approved Michigan's fourth Constitution with a thin 50.2-percent majority, 810,860-803,436. From the Charles L. Follo papers, box one, in the Michigan Historical Collections at the University of Michigan's Bentley Historical Library.

1966 'Cars poured in a steady stream'

Traffic, push-button phones amaze British visitor

Sir Miles Thomas, former chairman of British Overseas Air Corp., had seen more of the world than most people, and on a tour of the United States in 1966, he wrote about Detroit in a story for Britain's Western Mail newspaper.

Appropriately enough, Detroit is still the fastest of all the many cities of the world that I have visited in the past 12 months.

Equally appropriately, the main problem of Detroit in this day and age seems to be what to do with a motorcar when it is not motoring.

I looked down from my 17th-floor hotel window onto a huge car-park that was atop an eight-floor exhibition building — something like Earls Court with a flat roof.

Cars poured in a steady stream from the suburbs along a six-lane expressway. Those making for this particular location peeled off from their pre-selected right-hand lane and corkscrewed up a spiral ramp, taking several turns to reach the car-park level. Drivers paid their fees without completely stopping, handing their money in return for a ticket from one of several colored attendants, then sped across the rooftop to leave their cars in a neat herringbone pattern.

Those who were near it walked to an elevator that took them down to ground level; those who were farthest away waited for a little bus to take them to the elevator.

The philosophy of motor usage in Detroit is to maintain constant flow. There is no on-street parking. Roads and streets are regarded as pipelines, and the authorities do not believe in having them furred by stationary vehicles.

And while we in this country are exercised about the validity of a 70 m.p.h. maximum speed limit on our motorways, on the expressways in and around Detroit they impose minimum speed limits.

A great deal of thought has gone into making things easy, and therefore safe, for the motorist.

For instance, one drives out to the airport and while one airline porter takes away one's baggage, a car valet exchanges a ticket for the ignition keys, slips into the car and drives away to an area in which the car can either be washed or greased or both and kept ready for redelivery at the airport arrivals ramp when the returning traveler produces his ticket at the conclusion of his air trip.

Automated wash of cars is a thriving business in Detroit.

At the slightest flurry of snow — and for at least five months of the year that is to be expected — the streets are liberally coated with salt sprayed on briskly from huge tanker trucks. That gets rid of the snow and keeps the road surfaces free from ice, but it plays havoc with the underwork of cars, the metal corroding literally into holes in the body panels if it is left on for any length of time.

And so a dirty car is a quickly deteriorating car. A fast wash costs up to $10.

You drive the car to the entrance of what, on a cold day, looks like a steaming inferno, and while you sit in it, operators — rubber-suited like frogmen — with long spray nozzles slosh off the accumulated dirt, snow, ice and what-have-you and then, in a comparatively clear space, you are invited to get out, wind the windows up, leave the car in neutral with the brakes off, and it is attached to a moving conveyor where it is soused and squirted and flailed with mechanical mops, dried in a hot-air section, and delivered looking spotlessly clean and, to a degree, polished.

193

Tony Spina/Detroit Free Press

The ramp and rooftop parking at Cobo Hall in the 1960s.

Not only is fast living in cars practiced in Detroit. Telephones no longer have dials. Instead, on the instrument are 10 little buttons about half the size of the average typewriter key, arranged in three neat rows of three with the zero at the bottom. Letters of the alphabet have been completely replaced by numbers. This touch-button system is much, much faster than the rotating dial. And it needs to be, for even local numbers can involve up to 10 or 11 digits.

Living is not cheap in this pulsating womb of mass motorcar production.

But it is noticeably less expensive than, say, New York, and the end-of-season, last-year's type of motorcar, factory-fresh, can be bought for $10 deposit and no payment needed for the next two or maybe three months.

But with all this fast living one modern problem has not been overcome. The quality of television, both monochrome and color, is nothing like as good as our British standards for clarity of picture.

It was explained to me that there is so much building going on that as these tall steel cranes rise and their jobs swing round 24 hours a day hoisting steel framework and pouring concrete, the television waves bounce and cause bad drifting and color distortion.

Not that anybody really complains. Everybody lives too fast to look at a television set for more than a minute or two at a time. From which there may be something for us to learn, too.

Thomas' article was reprinted in the Aug. 7, 1966, issue of the Detroit Free Press Sunday magazine.

1967 *'The street was just mobbed'*

Detroit's riot as seen from an island in the river

A tense calm had settled on Detroit in the wake of the 1967 riots when Ruth E. Lee wrote to friends about the disturbances. She and her husband, Robert E. Lee, were the only legal residents of Belle Isle at the time, living above the Great Lakes Museum, where he was curator. She wrote this letter on July 31, a Monday.

The island was closed at 7 a.m. Sunday, July 23, after the riot on Twelfth Street had been going three or four hours. We didn't know it was closed or that anything had happened until our guide, Mr. Jackson, came upstairs and told us at about 11:30 a.m. We got up late and were having Sunday papers and coffee as usual. We immediately turned on police radio, which we follow pretty regularly, keeping track of the crime situation in Detroit. It was giving forth so much trouble it was impossible to keep up with it.

We kept turning on regular radio for news and all we could get was the Tiger ballgame on WJR and opera on WWJ. We found out later that one of the civil rights men had begged all stations to make no announcement, as they were pretty sure they could get things calmed down soon. Guess it was at least 3 p.m. or later before we heard anything and then not much.

As a result, the people at the ball game and many others drove home right into the worst of the riot. Among them our preparator, Pat Labadie, and his wife, who saw a fire in the distance and decided to go see what it was. They got on Grand River and the street was just mobbed with people — whole families looting. They had to drive down the turn lane and on the sidewalks, etc., to make it at all. Fortunately this riot — with some exceptions — was not like our 1943 one or they would be dead. People

Harry Wolf

Ruth and Robert E. Lee on a Great Lakes cruise aboard the S.S. South American in 1964.

ignored them. Pat's wife was hysterical when they realized what they had gotten into. Who wouldn't be?

I guess the most unbelievable thing we went through was standing out on the roof I think Sunday night — it gets to be a blur of

Tony Spina / Detroit Free Press

A soldier keeps his rifle ready as a building burns in Detroit

horror — and hearing a regular bombardment — like the finale of Hudson's fireworks, or perhaps Vietnam — and seeing a huge pink glow where buildings were burning a few blocks north of Jefferson Avenue — on Kercheval. This was DETROIT?

Tuesday we went out and looked over Kercheval in the afternoon and saw over a block of stores burned to the ground. Went up Woodward and saw one large building gone and dozens of windows broken where they had been looted. Three loan firms in one block had been broken into — and I can't say I feel bad — the way they cheated those poor people.

Tuesday night was worse and worse. Listened in on some of the reporters phoning their stations and heard them while they were actually under fire. Heard a little four-year-old girl had been shot — never did find out by whom for sure. Snipers more and more active.

Thursday began to be much more normal — some sniping, loot being discovered, reported by neighbors, etc.

Just like I never could really feel Saigon, or Newark or Watts, no one can understand the fear and sadness until he has been through it. We had only two or three hours of sleep a night for four days because we felt we should listen to the police radio — and the folks who were nearer didn't need a radio to know a war was going on.

Maybe some good will come out of it — but maybe the deep race hatred will only be deepened in those who have always had it.

Will anybody come to Belle Isle — even though it was the safest place in Detroit?

Let's hope we all find the answers to these awful problems.

Forty-three people died in the rioting and 657 were injured. It prompted community leaders to form New Detroit, with the aim of attacking discrimination head-on. Ruth E. Lee now lives in Sterling Heights and submitted this letter.

1975 *'Empty houses and stores'*

Recession strips Detroit to a gritty skeleton

Economic troubles were gnawing at Detroit in 1975 when Detroiter Lawrence Joseph commuted between the city and the University of Michigan Law School in Ann Arbor. Joseph kept a journal of events and his perceptions.

Jan. 15

Mid-January. "No hopeful signs for the economy." Detroit is hurting, badly; "as Detroit goes so goes the nation." More and more empty houses and stores, For Lease and For Sale signs. "As long as Supplemental Unemployment Benefits pay holds out" — but then what? And to think that two years ago one of the major issues in the shops was voluntary overtime!

Feb. 18

Dusk. At the river. No smoke from the two Uniroyal smokestacks — an eerie image against the dark gray light and the dark, green muddy river. I remember — it was nearly two years ago now — when I worked at the Chrysler Clairpointe factory, before I began law school. Standing on the loading dock with Bill Leuvanos, break time, the sun bright yellow, the upper half of the sky clear blue, the lower half its perpetual brown-dust color — burned earth. I said, "It's pretty today." Leuvanos replied, matter-of-factly, "Detroit is never pretty." I asked him to tell me, then, what kind of day it was. "Detroit is never pretty," he repeated.

Earlier this afternoon, at the Biff's Coffee Shop on Jefferson, an old woman, destitute, a tattered blue dress above her knees, red socks at her ankles, laughing at two policemen. Later, in Memorial Park, beside the river, the flock of waterfowl lifting in unison, first parallel to the river, then upward toward Lake St. Clair — the touch of warmer weather in the air. Smells of wet grass. River smells.

Paul Magnusson/Detroit Free Press
Lawrence Joseph in 1983

June 13

Last night, after dinner, a long drive through the east side. The constant blight — Van Dyke, Harper, Gratiot, Vernor. Mack Avenue: whole blocks as if bombed during an old war, never rebuilt. This is three or four miles from where we live. Then, out Gratiot northeast, the neighborhoods "at the outskirts" near Denby High: rows of small brick houses, well kept, with trimmed, handsome yards. Small stores, a lot of bars. Occasional For Sale signs.

Dec. 22

A day spent, mostly, riding buses — down Warren, downtown, then back, to get Nancy's ignition key because mine had broken in the frozen car lock. On the bus, the utter realization where I am. An old Irishman wearing a white shirt with a starched collar suddenly started to talk to me — within minutes I knew he was retired, that he worked in auto factories and small tool-and-die shops from 1925 to 1960, "been retired 16 years," and that he had never worked long enough at any one place to have received a pension. Waiting for the bus downtown near Crowley's, a 15-year-old girl, slightly cross-eyed, biting her lower lip self-consciously; she's ashamed how she looks. The old man waiting in line before me — waist-length naval jacket, small blue cap, unshaven, protruded jaw — every five minutes cursing, "The damn bus is late." We wait 30 minutes but it seems twice as long. The air turned cold — Detroit gray cold. The ride back, on Gratiot, hundreds of stores closed forever. Onto Warren, at the Chrysler Kercheval plant, a worker leaning from a third-story window, looking at the bus. Another worker gets off the bus, runs to the gate — he's late for work. A worker in his grease-stained apron on the loading dock, outside for a smoke — and memories when I would do the same. A "motor city:" Eventually we come to the factories. All of us — a girl, 18, on the bus reading "Crime and Punishment," the blessed, the f---offs, the respectable liars, the lost, the cool crooks — all of us, our lives are here.

Joseph is a lawyer, an associate professor of law at Hofstra University in Hempstead, N.Y., and a poet. From the Michigan Quarterly Review, spring 1986, University of Michigan: pages 296-302.

1986 *'Man is just beginning'*

At the end of one frontier, on the edge of the next

Snowed in at his remote home in AuTrain by an Upper Peninsula blizzard in late January 1986, Tom Avery wrote in his journal. He wrote about what he saw outside the window and on the television screen.

Jan. 26

The hoopla is over. Super Bowl XX is history, a bust, a 46-10 blowout . . . But what a spectacle! What an event!

One-hundred-twenty-five million people tuned in. Imagine that. I can't imagine 125 million of anything.

I stare out the window this morning and try to imagine 80 degrees!

Nothing is moving outside except wind and snow. The weatherman predicts clearing toward afternoon and temperatures of 18 to 20 below zero tonight. Imagine that!

Business shelled out a fortune yesterday, selling cars and trucks, McDLTs, lite beer, waterproof watches, truck-bed liners and putting the nation on the lookout for Herb, Burger King's lost-and-found nerd.

Even here, lost in the throes of a howling U.P. blizzard, I find myself living in an incredible era of communication, exploration, discovery and learning (?). I don't think the 125 million people who tuned in yesterday learned much, but media has its moments . . .

Away from the U.P. for six years, I am amazed at the number of satellite dishes that have popped up.

The world, our whole reality, is shrinking — and programmed live and in color *it's* being beamed everywhere.

My parents had been in Florida to watch Columbia lift off, its departure from earth delayed by weather.

Challenger is on the launching pad, but NASA had postponed yesterday's launch,

Courtesy Tom Avery

Tom Avery

scrubbed today's mission and wasn't sure about tomorrow — weather!

Everybody talks about it, but . . .

Jan. 27

From space, Voyager II, launched nine years ago, speeds on toward Neptune after "exploring" Uranus, discovering new moons, like Minerva — and rings — sending back pictures through two billion miles of empty blackness.

Scientists are picking up signals from Voyager; signals 1,000 times weaker than can be received by an ordinary radio, signals that travel at the speed of light, 186,000 miles per second, signals that take three hours to get here — and painting pictures of frontiers . . .

Jan. 28

The phone rang as I wrote.

"Are you watching the television or

listening to the radio?"

"No."

"The space shuttle blew up right after launch."

"Challenger? Thanks for calling. I'll get back with you."

I turned on the set and watched disaster replayed again and again.

Later, I read through my groping, exploratory, cabin-fever text.

Every word — thought — about frontiers, courage and daring, the wonder that drives men to know, had been blown right out of the sky, punctuated by a ball of fire and a trail of white smoke that just hung in the air like a leftover exclamation point.

Jan. 29

I've been snowed in for two days with no one to talk to, the only news the loss of Challenger and her crew.

I could scream!

I'm growing fitfully tired of Dan Rather.

It was inevitable. We all knew that sooner or later something like this was going to happen. But God, we didn't expect it!

As individuals, as a nation, the loss was devastating, but enough already!

We can watch that launch 100 times a day each day for the next year and it won't change what happened.

We may learn what happened, pinpoint a cause — but only God will ever know why . . .

Man is *just beginning* to wonder, still mustering the courage *to dare to challenge,* much less explore, the vast unknown . . .

But if you need seven people in order to go exploring, take me! If NASA could put another shuttle on the launching pad, ready to lift off tomorrow, I'd be there ready for the ride.

From Avery's "Rural Free Deliveries," Avery Color Studios, AuTrain, 1986: pages 60-63.

Index